CHAPTER 8

CHAPTER 7

CLASSIC GOLF INSTRUCTION

CLASSIC GOLF

INSTRUCTION

CHRISTOPHER OBETZ WITH MATTHEW RUDY

DRAWINGS BY ANTHONY RAVIELLI

RIZZOLI
NEW YORK

Note from the Author:

As a special thanks for your purchase, *Golf Digest* would like to offer a free one-year subscription for your golfing enjoyment. Please go to www.ravielli.com to register for your free subscription. The website also provides readers with golf tips and the opportunity to ask questions from our team of *Golf Digest* instructional experts. Please log on to www.ravielli.com, go to Classic Golf, and then golftips@ravielli.com to ask questions and share your thoughts.

Christopher Obetz

First published in the
United States of America in 2005
By Rizzoli International Publications, Inc.
300 Park Avenue South
New York, NY 10010
www.rizzoliusa.com

Reprinted 2006

2006 2007 2008 / 10 9 8 7 6 5 4 3 2

Design by Opto

ISBN-10: 0-8478-2690-2
ISBN-13: 978-0-8478-2690-2
Library of Congress Control Number:
2005924880

Printed in the United States

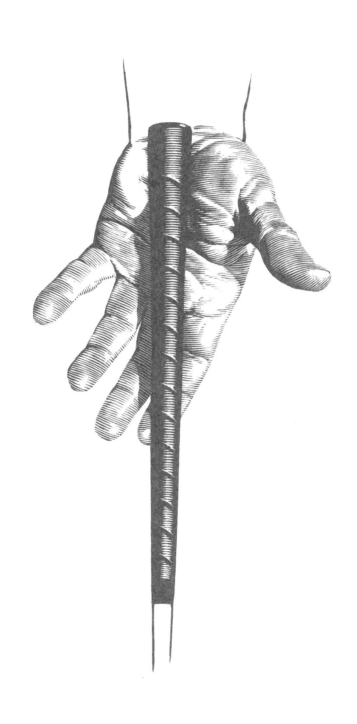

FOREWORD

BY JACK NICKLAUS

WHEN CHRISTOPHER first told me the story about his discovery of the original drawings of Anthony Ravielli, I couldn't help but think that the real find was for golfers everywhere. This chronology illustrating the fundamentals and nuances of golf technique might have been lost, but now, fortunately, current and future generations of golfers have the opportunity to enjoy and learn from these priceless drawings.

Christopher's father, Robin, was a childhood golf companion of mine, and I knew that he had taught Christopher all the beautiful subtleties of a game I consider the greatest of them all. From his father, Christopher inherited an appreciation and respect for the game at an early age. At the same time, Christopher's grandfather gave him a book, Ben Hogan's *Five Lessons: The Modern Fundamentals of Golf*, to serve as his first instructional guide to the game. His knowledge of the drawings that brought to life Hogan's work, combined with the nurturing he received in his youth, allowed Christopher to better understand the importance of Ravielli's works.

Seeing these remarkable drawings, Christopher immediately knew he had a responsibility for their preservation. In addition, he realized Ravielli's drawings had never been seen in their greatest glory as a full collection, nor had they been reproduced to the height of their potential. Now, we have such a body of work.

This collection is as timeless as the game itself. The pages of *Classic Golf Instruction* contain the single greatest compilation of golf instructional illustrations by artist Anthony Ravielli. Accompanying each image are time-honored traditions of fundamental golf instruction, along with the wisdom of golf's great teachers and players.

Ravielli's commitment to detail, anatomical accuracy, and his one-of-a-kind ability to visually convey the words, swings, and teachings of the golfers he observed represent true brilliance. Just as Bob Jones is an irreplaceable icon of the game's values and traditions, and just as Hogan is among the standards in instruction, Ravielli is the artistic equivalent.

As I have enjoyed seeing the original sketches of Jones and Hogan from their most revered books, along with those of hundreds of golf's memorable champions and teachers, my hope is that you likewise enjoy the Ravielli drawings first for their beauty and perfection. Secondly, may these drawings help you visualize the golf swing in your own quest to take on one of life's great challenges and pleasures.

Jack Nicklaus

INTRODUCTION

BY CHRISTOPHER OBETZ

SOME CONSIDER GOLF a game, light exercise in a pleasant setting. Some see it more as a form of meditation, an introspective challenge. To others, it is the ultimate test of mental and physical competition. For a sport that means many different things to many people, it should come as no surprise that from selecting a club, to understanding a lie, to getting out of trouble, there are virtually as many how-to methods and philosophies of strategy as there are golfers.

Golf has always been a part of my life. My father grew up down the street from Jack Nicklaus in Columbus, Ohio. They were friends and kindred spirits who walked the fairways of Scioto Country Club, shagged balls on the range, and discussed each shot until the evening sky grew dark and they could no longer follow the flight of the ball.

As my father recounted such stories, the passion in his voice was as though the game had been invented for the two of them to conquer, giving me a rich understanding of how deeply golf could affect a person's life. Though I never came close to mastering the sport even after numerous lessons from such legends as Jack Grout, Nicklaus's first teacher, my respect for my fellow golfers, the beauty of the surroundings, and the game's honor is the foundation of my golf experience.

Among those who share this passion, Anthony Ravielli stands apart. His love of the game no doubt was instrumental in attaining his status as golf's most revered instructional artist, sought after by luminaries like Ben Hogan, Bobby Jones, Byron Nelson, Sam Snead, and Tom Watson. Commonly referred to as the "Leonardo da Vinci of golf

Opposite: The author's father, Robin Obetz (second from left), played numerous rounds with Jack Nicklaus (second from right) at Scioto Country Club in Columbus, Ohio. Filling out this foursome are Bob Barton (far left) and Scioto head pro Jack Grout (far right).

instruction" because of the precise anatomical renderings of his work, Ravielli had the ability to transform the golf swing into easily understood drawings, a skill that won him fans and admirers around the world.

I count myself among the most passionate of his fans. When I was a child, my grandfather would give me golf books to read after Sunday night family dinner. Not a great golfer, a bogey player at best, he nonetheless loved the game and was one of its great students. His collection of books included hundreds of "how-tos." If there was a way to achieve the perfect swing, he was going to find it—or at least give it a try. From these shelves, *Five Lessons* was his choice for a hopeful young golfer's first read.

Like many before and since, I devoured Hogan's words and imprinted Ravielli's drawings into my golf psyche. Even before I knew Ravielli's name, his art became synonymous in my mind with classic golf instruction drawings.

Decades later, I was walking down Madison Avenue in New York City when I came upon an antique shop that had always captured my curiosity. The shop's second-floor windows were completely covered with merchandise, and the doorway was a mysterious side entrance.

Finally, I decided to see what was inside. There was nothing atypical about the shop, which had the usual offerings. French and English furnishings, paintings, tapestries, and possessions of all kinds waiting to be sold filled the rooms and corridors. But one room was different. It had an enormous billiard table with deep-green silk tassels hanging from the pockets. There were dozens of antique golf clubs scattered on the floor, along with an odd zebra-striped golf bag.

Perhaps, I thought, I could find a Christmas present for my father, who always appreciates golf memorabilia or a good cigar. Poking around, I came upon some boxes on the floor, filled with what appeared to be golf drawings on heavy white boards. Picking one up, I immediately recognized the artist's hand. The unmistakable style immediately jogged my memory; I knew I had seen these many years ago.

Then it hit me.

Barely touching these masterpieces, I sifted through the inventory. Could this be? Yes, it was. The lessons and history of golf as witnessed and documented by Anthony Ravielli.

There were hundreds of scratchboards, as well as original sketches and manuscripts from *The Basic Golf Swing*, on which Jones had made handwritten edits on the typed text.

The box also contained the original cover illustration for *Five Lessons: The Modern Fundamentals of Golf*, arguably the most famous piece of golf art ever created—*Five Lessons* is in its 64th printing, making it the most-read golf instruction book of all time. To think this collection might have been lost, forgotten, or broken up was foremost on my mind. Preservation, to keep the collection intact so future generations would be able to observe and try for themselves these timeless techniques, became my primary objective.

Then, an additional discovery led my thoughts down another path. On the back of each sketch board was a studio stamp with an address and phone number: Stamford, Connecticut, a short commute by train from New York City. I loved Ravielli's art, but I knew nothing about the man. It was time to find out.

Nervous and full of questions, I called the number. "Hello, may I help you?" came the cheerful greeting. I introduced myself and asked to speak with Mr. Ravielli. After a pause, I was informed he had died in 1997, at the age of 86. I immediately felt a huge loss; the man responsible for these works was not available. How was I to find out more? I explained my interest in the history of golf and, in particular, the works of Ravielli. As sunny as the day, Mrs. Ravielli began to answer my questions.

Georgia, as she immediately wanted to be addressed, couldn't have been more open about her husband's life, and by the end of our 30-minute conversation, I knew I had to meet her. I wanted to learn about Ravielli's thoughts, his background, the beginnings, where he developed his amazing talent, and what it was like to work with the heroic figures of golf. Only Georgia could shed light on his inspiration, dreams, and fears.

After taking a train to Stamford, I got in a cab, which took me along a road winding through fieldstone walls and a wilderness of trees. Carrying her favorite sandwiches, egg salad, and a box of William Pole sugar cookies with berry centers, I was anxious to meet the woman behind the man and cull the memories of the man behind the woman.

The address was at the end of a cul-de-sac, a split-level with no apparent front door. Circling the house looking for a point of entry, I noticed an open window with a full

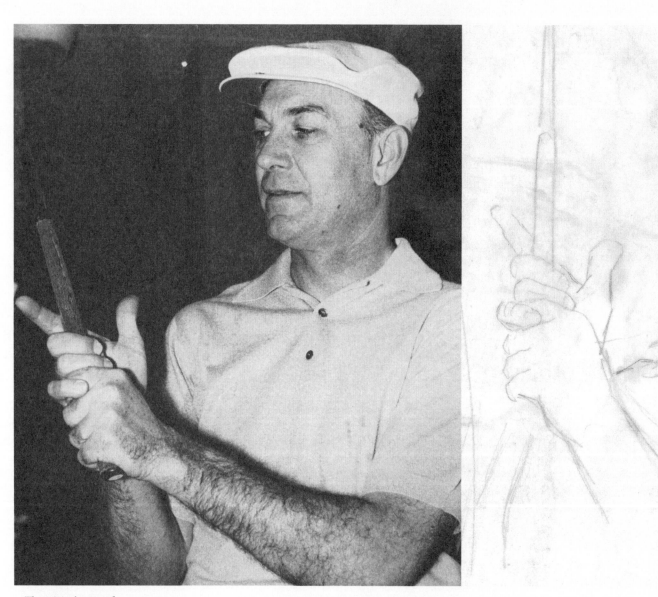

The original cover of
Ben Hogan's *Five Lessons*
came together in three
stages: photograph, sketch,
scratchboard.

skeleton hanging beside a desk inside. I was curious, but I didn't want to seem impolite and peer inside, so I proceeded to look for what would be my best guess as the front door. After several knocks, Georgia, a small woman in a housedress holding a cigarette, opened the door with the warmest of smiles and invited me in.

I could feel Ravielli's presence from my first step inside the house. As Georgia and I began to talk, sharing our sandwiches and little bits about ourselves, we felt an immediate bond.

Our shared passion was her husband. She had fallen in love with him more than 40 years before, and I was to fall in love with him that day. Over the next several hours, the picture of the artist and the man, known always as Tony to golf legends and neighbors alike, came together.

Georgia revealed details of their lives. As she would tend to matters of family—the Raviellis had three children, Jane, Ellen, and Tony, Jr.—Tony, Sr., a night owl, would work in his home studio from 5 p.m. through the night, until the kids got up to go to school. While he drew, she read. The consummate man seeking knowledge, he would give her books on anatomy, philosophy, and science for their dinner conversations.

Working at home, Tony was able to participate in raising his children. The kids were always welcome in his studio. Sometimes, he would wake them up at night if he were having a problem visualizing a particular pose. He would drape them in fabric to see exactly how the cloth and anatomy integrated. It was a happy household in which the kids came first. Georgia could only remember one instance in which Tony had ever raised his voice.

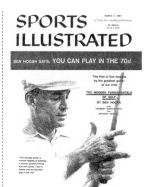

In fact, the family bond was so strong that when Tony's eyes began failing and cataract surgery was the only option, the family, as one, decided to use the college fund to restore Tony's sight. Everyone was generous of spirit and love. Tony made sure the bookshelves were filled, and dinner conversations centered around answers to the how and why questions of life.

Ravielli's efficiency allowed him to illustrate weekly golf tips for *Sports Illustrated*.

Tony's interest in science and art began early, and he was 5 when he knew he was to be an artist. Gathered on the sidewalks of New York City's Italian Harlem neighborhood with his friends, Tony would draw nature scenes of landscapes, dinosaurs, and people with colored chalk. His street art astonished pedestrians, and his friends would pass a hat, collecting pennies for afternoon sodas and enough chalk for Tony to continue the enterprise the following day.

Tony's father, a marine engineer and amateur wood-carver, deeply influenced and supported his son's artistic pursuits, all the way through his formal education at Cooper Union and the Art Students League. As a teenager, Tony's interest in nature turned into a fascination with the human body, and he fed his curiosity in an unorthodox way, at least for an aspiring artist.

Bypassing the classic training of studio rendering and figure drawing, Tony learned anatomy in the morgue at Bellevue Hospital, where he volunteered. As if he were one of the pupils in Rembrandt's *Anatomy Lesson of Dr. Tulp*, Tony's study of anatomy was more that of a medical student than an aspiring artist. But his method paid off. Tony's experiences at Bellevue helped perfect his knowledge of the human form, his greatest strength, and his obsession with the connection of muscles, bones, and their movements later enabled him to depict athletes in action as accurately as possible.

Tony also continued to study anatomy throughout his career, often using the American Museum of Natural History as a resource—the Hall of Human Biology provided generations of New York's great physicians, as well as a single inimitable artist, with the details of nature's complex creatures. Often taking his children with him, Tony would spend days sketching the exhibitions of fossil mammals and skeletal structures and reading in the museum's vast library before returning to his studio and illuminating his works with the mysteries and curiosities of the living form.

Tony's preferred medium, scratchboard, is now one of the most rarely used because of its complexity and the skill required. But the technique, which involves etching into the ink-layered board using thousands, perhaps of tens of thousands, of tiny, meticulous cuts, is so effective because of the realistic detail conveyed. Few artists before or since have

been able to master this art form as well as he could. Tony was remarkably prolific and versatile. For decades, he entered hundreds of thousands of Americans' homes regularly, first as an illustrator of a weekly golf-tip column for *Sports Illustrated* from 1955 to 1961, then in a similar capacity for the monthly *Golf Digest* from 1962 to 1990.

When not working on golf projects, Tony created children's books and worked with other extraordinary athletes and individuals who sought Tony for his mastery of illustrating the human form.

According to Georgia and his daughters, Tony's children's books fed his soul, and he dedicated himself to opening up the eyes of all children, not just his own. In *What Are Street Games?*, Tony reached back into his childhood and his first memories of being an artist, using his experiences to inspire his own children as well as many others.

Among Tony's other notable children's books are *The World Is Round*, *Rise and Fall of the Dinosaur*, *Elephants: Last of the Land Giants*, *From Fins to Hands*, *An Adventure in Geometry*, and *Around the World with Darwin*.

Tony's sophisticated style also resonated with an adult audience. He developed a close friendship with Isaac Asimov while collaborating on *The Wonders of the Human Body* and *The Human Body: Its Structure and Operation*. The two men shared a keen interest in explaining how the human body works.

In 1958, Tony worked with Don Carter, the most famous bowler of the day, on *Don Carter's 10 Secrets of Bowling*. After that, Tony would go on to write and illustrate *What Is Tennis?* In all, he published more than 100 books, including solo efforts and collaborations.

However, Hogan's *Five Lessons: The Modern Fundamentals of Golf* is the hallmark of Tony's career. Previously, golf instruction had been one-on-one. *Five Lessons* brought golf instruction to the masses and signaled the beginning of modern instruction methods, showing teachers and players they now had an outlet to share their wisdom to a large audience through Tony's superior knowledge of form and anatomy.

When Hogan, Tony, and ghostwriter Herbert Warren Wind teamed up on the project, each brought his own unique gift, which complemented the others' skills perfectly:

Hogan's intimate knowledge of golf mechanics; Wind's ability to translate Hogan's ideas into clear, readable prose; and Tony's skill in transforming Hogan's words into images in a way never before imagined.

There is no better example of Tony's genius and his key role in the process than the way the classic image of Hogan depicting swing plane with a pane of glass came together.

In Curt Sampson's *Hogan*, Wind says, "Ravielli was really the key player. Hogan looked at Tony's roughs—which he did in pencil—and said, 'My God, Tony, I've never seen anything like this. We've really got something here.'" Never before seen, these sketches show what excited Hogan: the stages in the development of the most famous image in golf instruction.

The success of *Five Lessons* made Tony the go-to illustrator for the last half of the 20th century, and he brought to life the techniques of some of golf's biggest names, including Bobby Jones and Tom Watson, in their books, not to mention hundreds of others for *Golf Digest*. Working with monthly deadlines, the magazine could rely on Tony to deliver on time polished works that needed few, if any, revisions. Even as photography became widespread, Tony was able to depict nuances and detail that photographs had a hard time capturing.

He often went on location to meet the players, photographing, sketching, and taking notes that would serve as a guide. A good golfer, Tony knew what the reader needed. "My main objective is to be as clear as possible," he once said. "I've played enough golf to know that in instruction you can't be a Rembrandt, and fail if you aren't easily understood."

Despite his decades of success, Tony never changed, inside or out. His wardrobe remained constant, consisting of comfortable flannel shirts that were as soft as the person inside them, and he always saw himself as the curious artist studying anatomy at Bellevue or reading textbooks to obtain more knowledge, simply blessed to earn a living and provide for his family by doing what he loved.

"Nothing really changed [after *Five Lessons*]," Georgia said that day between bites of egg salad. "Tony never considered himself famous. He took all his jobs seriously and was thrilled to be able to pursue his craft. It was his dream to make a living as an artist. He fulfilled that dream until his death."

Ravielli was able to use his experience and skill to illustrate what lay under the surface of the human skin.

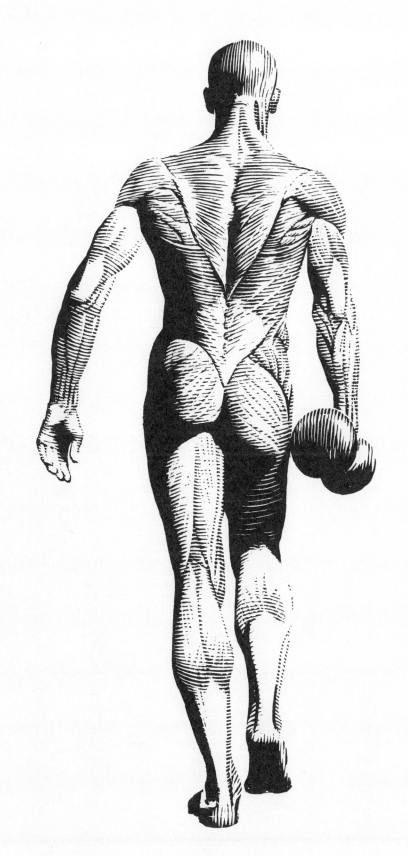

Part IV   The PLANE

II 1

40°

40°

drawing of
Hogan with
Piece of flat
cardboard

Check width
between panes

Ravielli played an impor-
tant role in developing
Hogan's pane-of-glass image
of swing plane for *Five
Lessons.* Upon seeing these
sketches, Hogan said, "My
God, Tony. We've really got
something here."

After several hours of conversation, I asked if it would be possible to see Tony's studio. Until seeing the desk and skeleton from outside as I was searching for the door, I had not known he worked from home. The question brought our first uncomfortable moment of the day. Although my curiosity was high, I could sense something was wrong and didn't push. As Georgia lit another cigarette and sank deeply into herself, I reassured her that it was fine if there was a reason she didn't want me to see the studio. My sense was that too many memories were left in that room, and she wasn't prepared to confront them.

She replied that she had ventured into his studio only several times in the seven years since Tony's death. With that response, I could appreciate their closeness and her profound sense of loss. For years before they met, Georgia would walk home from work late at night and wonder about the only light in the neighborhood that was always on. One day, she showed up at Tony's studio with a friend who was modeling for him. There was an instant attraction that lasted for the rest of his life. The purity of their connection was one I had only felt a few times previously.

After some contemplation, she decided it was time to visit his studio again, and we would do it together. Perhaps opening the door would be easier with someone next to her to provide comfort. We went down the stairs, Georgia turned the tarnished brass handle of the maple door, and we entered Tony's sanctuary.

The room looked much as I imagine it did while he was working on one of his masterpieces. "Skelly," a real skeleton of an unidentified Asian man, hung next to the wooden, slant-backed desk. His dental tools, used to make the legendary scratchboards of golfers, were still on his desk. The mirror he looked into for 40-plus years studying his facial movements reflected only his absence. All around were towers of books, stacks of scratchboards, and galleys. Only Tony himself was missing, although I could feel his spirit still at work.

After finding a lightbulb for me to screw in, Georgia departed rather quickly. She said I could look around, and she would wait upstairs. But I didn't spend much time in the studio. Concerned about Georgia and wanting to comfort her, I went back upstairs, knowing I would return again.

Her previous trips to the office with her daughter Ellen had been out of necessity: to remove the illustrations and protect them from the dampness that would have consumed such important artifact's in golf history. Prior to my discovery in the antique shop on Madison Avenue, the scratchboards had passed through several hands. Now, entering a world I was just beginning to know, I could see there was even more to protect.

In what some might consider a dream realized, Tony had the opportunity not only to document the fundamentals of golf instruction with the most renowned golfers but also share intimately in their personal experiences and innermost thoughts about the game. It was from these private moments that Tony was able to re-create their visions into renderings for all golfers to study and replicate. Within his drawings lie not only the game's secrets but also its beauty.

I walked upstairs and sat down again with Georgia. I knew it was difficult to stir up all the memories, but she reminded me the memories were only the best. He loved his children, he loved knowledge, and he loved her. I asked what Tony would want to be remembered for, and she said, "detail and authenticity." These qualities were evident throughout his art, and now I could see them in the way he lived as a husband and father.

Ultimately, Anthony was not just an artist. Whether communicating in person to his family, or through a book or magazine to adults, kids, golfers, bowlers, or aspiring doctors, he was an educator, an extraordinary talent, and a one-of-a-kind, world-class man.

ALWAYS ON TARGET

BY NICK SEITZ

YOU CAN ARGUE long into the night about golf's all-time best player or best teacher or best course designer. But there is no argument about the game's finest instruction artist ever. That has to be the late Anthony Ravielli, the first artist to win a major award for outstanding work in golf journalism.

I had the pleasant privilege of working with Tony for more than 25 years as the editor of *Golf Digest* and the collaborating writer on Tom Watson's how-to books, one of which, *Getting Up and Down*, made a brief visit to the best seller list, in no small part due to Tony's role.

Many painstaking hours went into the books. Watson is a perfectionist, and so was Tony, who also served as the ground wire for our little group—consistently calm, adaptable, creative.

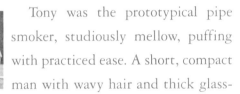

Above: Ravielli, Tom Watson, and Nick Seitz (left to right) were frequent collaborators. Watson provided the ideas, Seitz the words, and Ravielli the unforgettable images.

Tony was the prototypical pipe smoker, studiously mellow, puffing with practiced ease. A short, compact man with wavy hair and thick glasses, he wore patterned cotton shirts with the sleeves rolled up, ready to work for as long as necessary. He was not easy to work with; he was a delight to work with.

Says Tony Wimpfheimer, then managing editor of Random House, which published *Up and Down*, "I always felt Tony worked best with others of his same passion—superstars like Watson and [Ben] Hogan and [Bobby] Jones. He was right there on the same plane with them."

Many was the time Watson would pore over a rough (first sketch) of an intricate subject such as the

Even in the age of photography, Ravielli's artistic
methods were more effec-
tive in communicating golf
technique, as in this example showing the differences
in the setup and swing with
an iron and driver.

grip, then jump up from the table to take Tony's hands and demonstrate a subtle adjustment he wanted to convey. Watson never had to show Tony twice. (The joke at *Golf Digest* was that Tony's roughs were more polished than most artists' finished work.)

Tony would pore over a manuscript several times to be sure he grasped a golfer's thinking, then talk to him to make sure what the player saw in his mind's eye matched what Tony saw in his swing. Tony wanted to know what a move felt like to the player, because that could lead to surprising imagery.

He said the top players were like scientists in the way they studied the game. "Illustrating golf technique is like doing medical illustrations," he would say. "You can't fake it." Tony always said anatomy was his first love. A full skeleton hung in his office for reference.

Working in an era when photography was coming of age, Tony's work—especially his scratchboard work—always stood out. Its anatomical precision (revealing muscular detail beneath the skin if called for, as in the Hogan art), highlighting of key points, and lyrical appeal were timeless. No camera could match Tony's imaginative rendering of

a timeworn idea with startling freshness.

His scratchboard style had no forerunner, no peer, and no successor in golf illustrating. Perhaps the difficulty of the technique and Tony's mastery of it discouraged competition. He was told he was the only artist handling active figures with that technique. He seems to have retired the genre. After Tony's passing, *Golf Digest* searched far and fruitlessly for a replacement, in the medical art fraternity and beyond, without a hint of luck.

Tony played golf and understood the game's technical nuances and terminology. He knew whereof he drew: He could show a swing position with confident familiarity, and even convey motion on an inert page.

Bobby Jones marveled at that facility when he wrote of Tony's artwork in *The Basic Golf Swing*: "To me, the drawings make the book. I think they are more revealing than photographs, because in them is expressed the artist's interpretation of the movement, as well as my own. Although each drawing illustrates a position, it also is capable of indicating whence the position was derived and in what direction will be the departure."

Tony said he enjoyed all the golf superstars he worked with, but enjoyed Jones the most. "He was a great guy despite being crippled with that terrible disease [syringomyelia, which afflicts the central nervous system]," he told me some years ago. "He knew he was dying. He was shriveled, and his hands were permanently clamped, but his mind was acutely sharp, and he was unfailingly pleasant and helpful. It was just the two of us in his office in Atlanta, and I treasured the experience.

"Cigarettes were lined up on his desk in holders," Tony remembered. "His secretary would light one and put it in his mouth, then he could handle it with his knuckles. I developed the concept for *The Basic Golf Swing* and whipped up a dummy that pleased him. I told him to be as severe in his reactions as he could. He said not to show him too many things too often or he'd keep changing them. 'If you want to tell me to go to hell,' he said, 'please feel free.' He approved every piece of art in the book, but there weren't many changes. His basics were as strict as Hogan's, though Jones was more rhythm-minded. He made and kept a lot of notes and was an exceptionally good writer—the best of any player.

"My only regret is that I never had a picture taken with Jones."

Great golfers appreciate consummate professionalism when they meet it in people outside their own vocation and are, somewhat surprisingly given their requisite strong egos, willing to cooperate with it and even defer to it. All the superstars Tony worked with—Jones, Hogan, Sam Snead, Byron Nelson, et al.—respected him and his art without reservation.

He also won the respect and admiration of his peers in journalism. The Met Golf Writers Association honored him with the prestigious Lincoln Werden Journalism Award, a distinction he shares with the likes of Dan Jenkins, Dave Anderson, and Jim McKay.

Tony's art style, like his persona, was straightforward and unfreighted by frippery. What you see is all you need to see. He strived for, and achieved, clarity in its most distilled state. Listening to him talk about drawing was like listening to Ella Fitzgerald talk about singing.

"I try to be as economical as possible, and never embellish for effect," he once told me. "My style comes from trying to be emphatically clear and in control of the medium, whether it be scratchboard or watercolor or whatever."

From that you might infer that Tony's stuff is clean and precise but not particularly attractive or entertaining. You shouldn't. It is as aesthetically pleasing as it is instructive, as this splendid collection shows.

When Tony added highlighting to a piece, it invariably served to heighten the dramatic effect—to capture and focus the reader's attention. It might be circling a key emphasis, or using spot color, an arrow, or a dotted line. Never does it seem extraneous or showy or forced.

His imaginative use of imagery also transcended the ordinary. I think of a Watson tip on sand play in which Watson had to stand outside the bunker and bend severely at the waist to make the swing. Tony predictably depicted Watson's torso bent nearly to horizontal, but unpredictably added a color outline of a ghost hand holding down his head. The ghost hand turned a solid tip into a memorable one.

Another example: Watson wanted to make a point about choking down to the same point on different chipping clubs, to standardize the feel of the stroke. Tony telescoped the shafts of four different irons, essentially leaving just the hands, grips, and clubheads in a balanced row. A fresh look that came across at a glance.

The only criticism of his work I ever heard was from an art director who thought it old-fashioned. Tony would have taken that as a compliment. He never tried for trendy, correctly feeling that golf instruction was not the forum for it.

For all his talent and repute, he was remarkably self-effacing. Urged to sign his work more boldly, he never did. Over all the years working with him, I cannot recall a single tense moment. I was musing about that recently with Ken Bowden, who cowrote *Methods of Golf's Masters* and *Practical Golf*, both illustrated by Tony.

"His success never turned him into an egomaniac as it does so many people," Bowden said. "He was tougher on himself than any editor or author ever was, and he remained modest and down-to-earth through all our many dealings. He preferred photo references he shot himself, but he could produce superb work out of thin air. He was truly an illustrator rather than simply a tracer or copier as so many of his competitors were and are. I very much wish he was still among us."

This beautiful book lets us revisit Tony's eloquent work, which promises to live on in golf lore.

CLASSIC GOLF INSTRUCTION

GRIP | 1 |

INSTRUCTION BY
CHUCK COOK AND
DAVID LEADBETTER

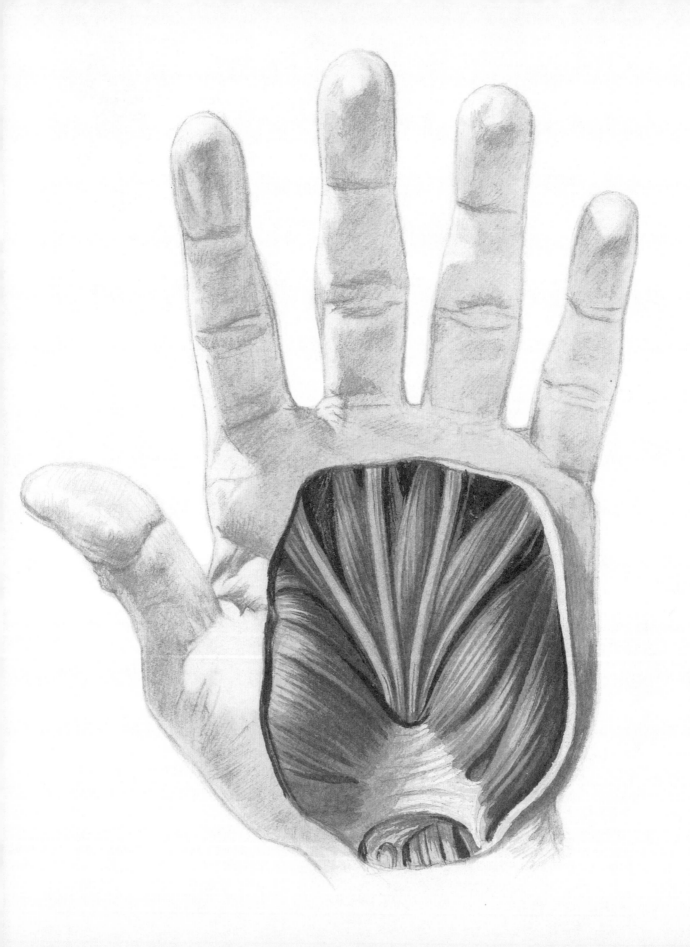

GRIP | 1

INSTRUCTION BY
CHUCK COOK AND
DAVID LEADBETTER

HANDS ARE A GOLFER'S greatest asset. Thick or thin, delicate or beefy, the hands are the epicenter of the swing, radiating out to the club and to the muscles, including the one my grandfather called the most important muscle, the brain.[Fig. 1.1] Everything in golf, good and bad, is an outgrowth of the grip, and a good one makes the club a complete extension of the body.

Anthony Ravielli illustrated this precise connection between the hands and the grip in this series of hand studies showing the meticulous way Ben Hogan places his right hand on the club. With the left hand firmly in place yet never applying too much pressure—a delicate balance—Hogan places the right hand over the left so the pinky finger of the right hand nestles between the index and middle finger of the left. When performed correctly, the right hand rests gently in place while the left hand remains in control.[Fig. 1.2]

Besides showing the way the hands fit against each other and onto the grip, Ravielli strove to fully understand how the hands move during the swing. In the drawing of Eddie Williams on the right, Ravielli skillfully isolated the grip at five different positions during the swing: setup and impact, takeaway, halfway back, postimpact, and follow-through.[Fig. 1.3]

1.1 Opposite: By understanding what lay beneath the surface, Ravielli's depiction of golf instruction was unsurpassed.

In the previous series, Hogan demonstrated the overlapping grip, the most popular of the three main styles; the others are the interlocking and baseball, or 10-finger, grip. In a more refined and romantic style, Ravielli used colored pencils to demonstrate how these grips are different.[(Fig. 1.4)]

In the interlocking grip, the right pinky locks between the index and middle fingers of the left hand instead of resting on top. This grip feels more secure for players with shorter fingers. Less common than the overlapping grip, it is nevertheless the choice of Jack Nicklaus and Tiger Woods.

The 10-finger grip features all the fingers on the club, as opposed to linking or overlapping. This hold is most popular among juniors, seniors, women, or anyone looking for more control during the swing.

For their differences, what these grips have in common is how the hands work as a single unit—especially at the top of the backswing, when players with poor grips often lose control of the club. These illustrations of Fay Crocker show how the left thumb fits snugly along the lifeline of the right hand, forming a bond that allows the hands to retain control of the club at the top.[(Fig. 1.5)]

Ravielli first became enchanted by the human form as a young man studying anatomy at Bellevue Hospital in New York City. He was fascinated by what lay beneath the skin, and it was his ability to depict the muscles in their everyday use that separated his illustrations from others and led him to become the most revered instructional artist of the last century.

Known for his perfectionism, Hogan sought out an artist whose illustrations of his swing would be as precise as the swing itself. Ravielli's fascination with anatomy made him the perfect candidate to become Hogan's illustrative muse. As Hogan became recognized for his clearly detailed instruction techniques, Ravielli became known as the only man capable of capturing the movement of the club, the skin, the inner workings of each muscle, the clothes, and the personalities of each golfer.

In addition to showing the grip in motion, Ravielli also placed the grip in a larger context in his drawings of Tom Watson's backswing and in a tip about touching the wrists in the follow-through for better accuracy.[Fig. 1.6/1.7]

To help you check for yourself whether your grip is correct, Ravielli illustrated an open left hand with shaded areas emphasizing the area of the palm and fingers where each golfer should feel the greatest pressure from the club.[Fig. 1.8] To truly understand the feeling, try closing your eyes and swing, focusing on where your hand and club connect.

Ravielli also used imagery to illustrate proper technique. Graham Post demonstrates that the proper left-hand grip pressure, applied with the last three fingers, is akin to the sensation of pouring water from a pitcher.[Fig. 1.9] By relating the golf swing to familiar objects and motions, Ravielli helped the new golfer visualize and ingrain proper technique. Before moving ahead in *Classic Golf Instruction*, take the time to familiarize yourself with the grip and develop a relationship with the club. It will make your journey in golf much smoother.

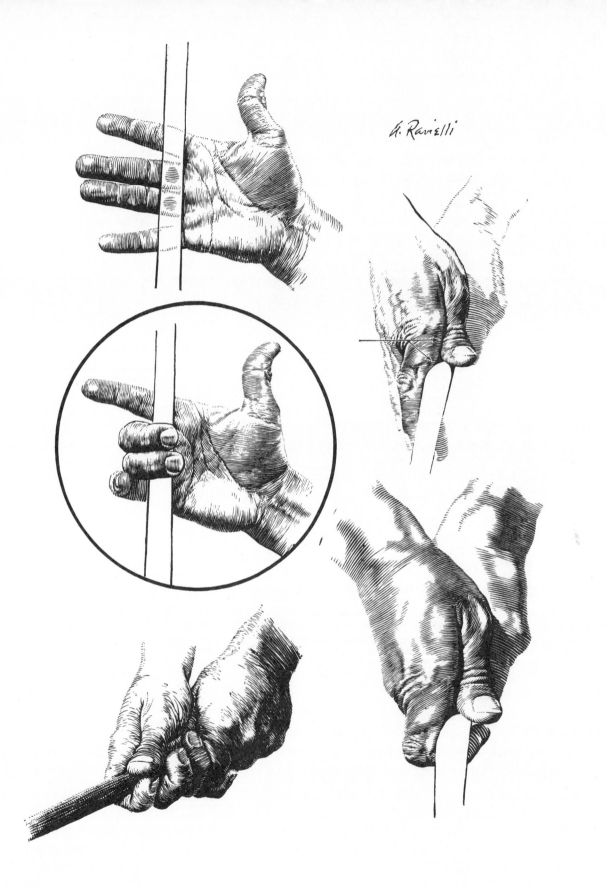

G. Ravielli

1.3 Ravielli was able to isolate the hands, to show how they should work at different points during the swing.

1.2 Opposite: Always meticulous, Ben Hogan demonstrates the process of placing his hands precisely on the club. When performed correctly, the right hand rests gently in place while the left hand remains in control.

1.4 Ravielli used a different
medium, colored pencils, to
demonstrate the three main
types of grips: overlapping,
interlocking, and 10-finger
or baseball grip.

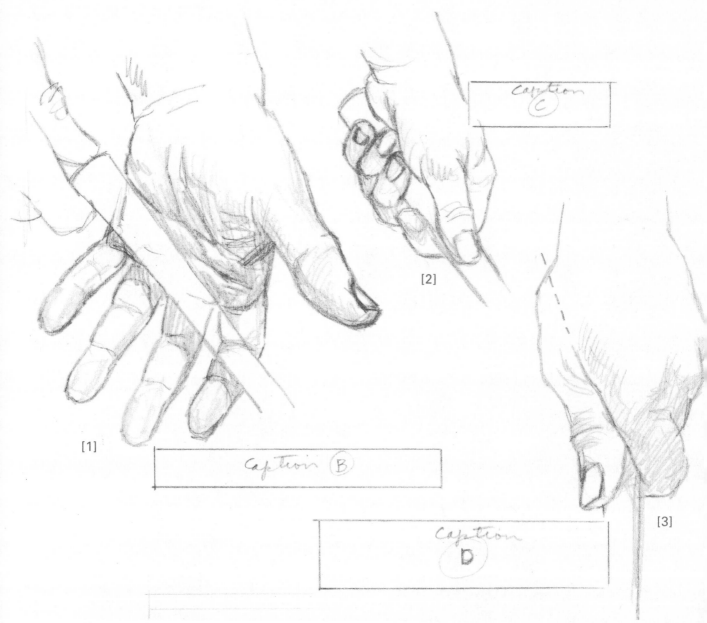

[1]

Caption (B)

[2]

Caption (C)

[3]

Caption (D)

THE GRIP The purpose of the grip is twofold: to square the club-face when in the ideal impact position, and to allow the wrist to hinge correctly. To perform both tasks, here is a step-by-step lesson on how to place your hands on the grip.

THE LEFT-HAND GRIP [1] By placing the heel pad on top of the grip, you're able to create the necessary leverage to cock the wrists. [2] When the club is held properly, in the fingers, the tips of the fingers will just touch the base of the thumb. [3] Placing the left thumb halfway between the top of the grip and the side of the grip will make it easier to square the clubface, in the ideal impact position.

THE RIGHT-HAND GRIP [4] The club is held more in the fingers of the right hand because the hand has to wrap around both the grip and the left thumb. The right hand should face the target, with the lifeline covering the left thumb. This puts both hands in position to allow the wrists to hinge freely. [5] This is an overlapping grip, with the pinky finger of the right hand overlapping the index finger of the left hand. In an interlocking grip, these two fingers would intertwine. [6] A good grip check is to look for two knuckles of the left hand and one of the right hand. Also, the ends of the Vs created by the thumb and side of each hand will align with each other over the middle of the club's handle and point between your right ear and shoulder. –CHUCK COOK

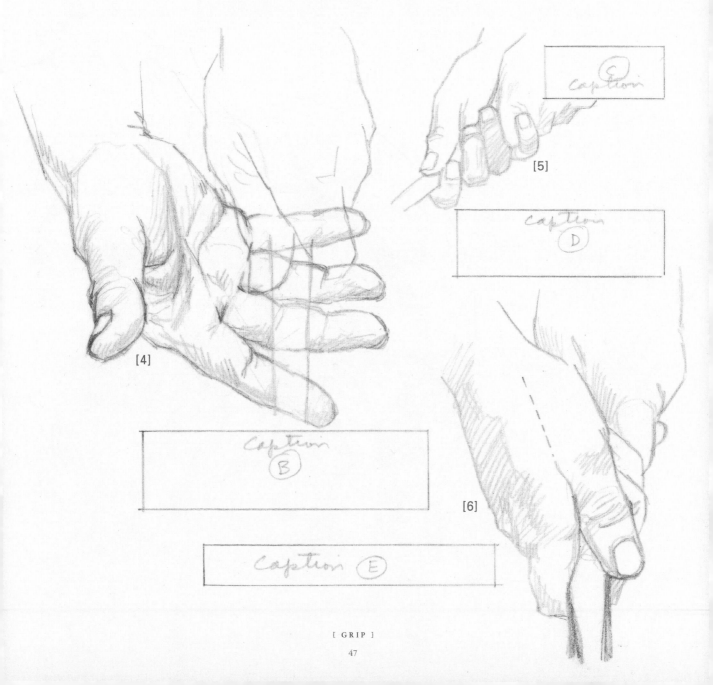

[4]

[5]

caption C

caption D

caption B

[6]

Caption E

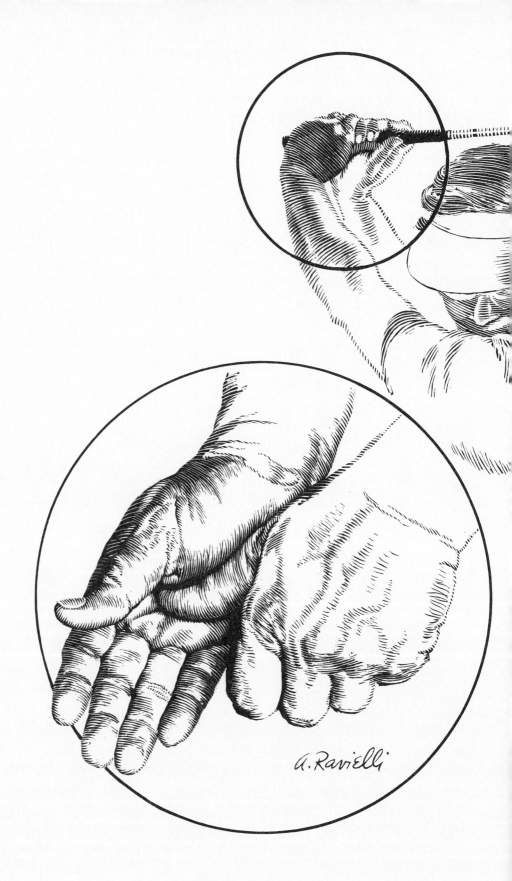

1.5 Fay Crocker shows
how the left thumb
fits snugly in the right
palm, forming a union
that enables the golfer to
retain control of the club
throughout the swing.

1.6 The proper release with
a good grip means the
forearms will touch in the
follow-through.

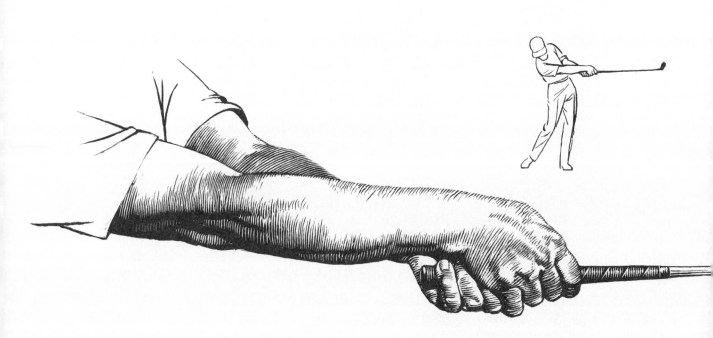

1.7 Notice how solidly
Tom Watson's hands
support the club halfway
back in the backswing.

A. Ravielli

TAKE THE GRIP IN FRONT OF YOU Anthony Ravielli's drawings
bring Ben Hogan to life. The incredible attention to detail, faithful representation of the human body, and correct form make them something more—still pictures with rhythm. They show even more life
than the original Hogan photographs Mr. Ravielli used as reference.

I spent months studying those photographs and used them in
my own instruction book *The Fundamentals of Hogan*. The drawings that came from those photographs have an almost three-
dimensional quality. This drawing shows Hogan demonstrating
grip pressure. I used an original photograph from this series for the
cover of my book. It's impressive how Ravielli was able to re-create
Hogan's grip, right down to the veins and creases in the skin.

Hogan is demonstrating how finger pressure isn't constant
throughout the grip—it should be lighter through the middle, in the
index finger of the left hand and the last finger of the right hand,
and in the right thumb and index finger. Hogan wasn't forming his
grip in front of his body just for demonstration purposes, either.
Most players never really look at how they set the grip. They grip
the club with their hands below the waist and go from there.
Hogan was always setting and resetting his grip with his hands in
front of him, so he could make sure it was correct—even though he
hit hundreds of balls a day. That's a good lesson for the rest of us.
–DAVID LEADBETTER

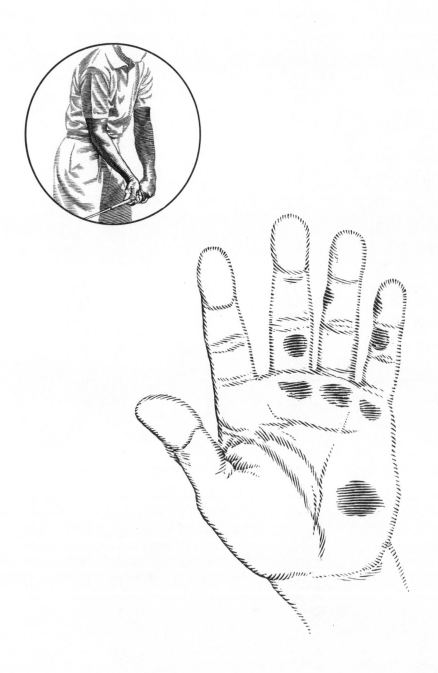

1.8 It is possible to tell
whether your grip is correct
by the pressure points
between the hand and
the club.

1.9 The correct grip pressure is similar to the pressure needed to pour water from a pitcher.

G. Ravielli

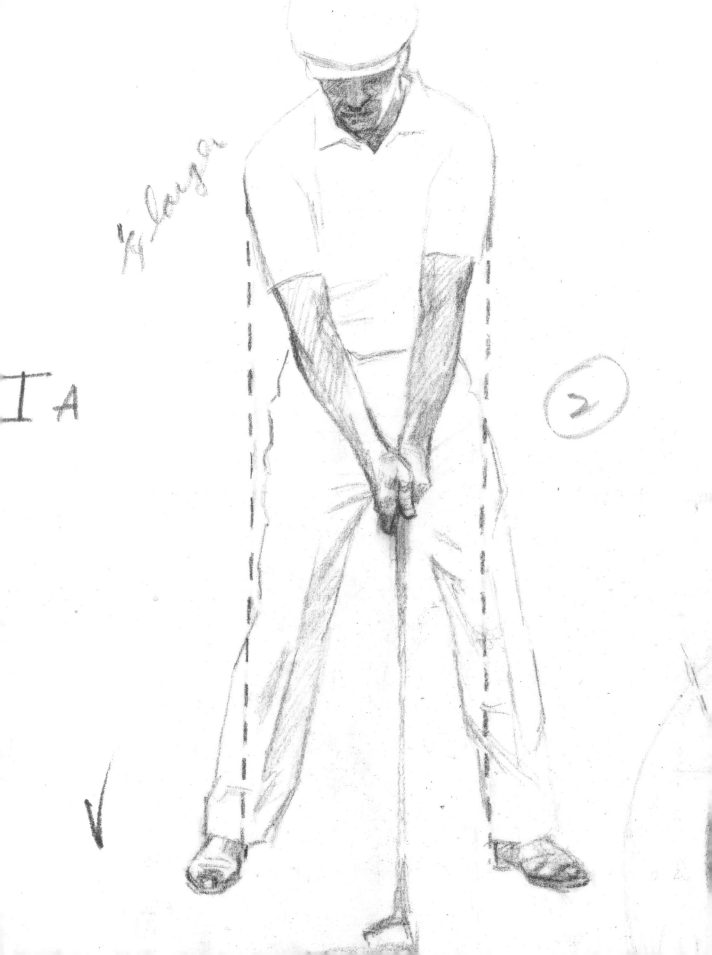

I A

¾ larger

SETUP |2|

INSTRUCTION BY
GREG NORMAN AND
BUTCH HARMON

SETUP |2|

INSTRUCTION BY
GREG NORMAN AND
BUTCH HARMON

JACK NICKLAUS ARTICULATED the importance of setup best when he wrote, "If you set up correctly, there's a good chance you'll hit a reasonable shot, even if you make a mediocre swing. If you set up to the ball poorly, you'll hit a lousy shot even if you make the greatest swing in the world."

Even among the game's greats, there is a certain amount of variety in swing technique, from Nicklaus's upright action to Ben Hogan's flat plane, from Nick Price's quick swing to Ernie Els's smooth, languid tempo. Yet all these champion golfers start from roughly the same address position, with some margin for personal preferences and differences in build.

Keep that in mind as you study the following illustrations Ravielli produced for *Sports Illustrated*'s "Tips from the Top," among others. Although he showed a variety of setup examples, he also was able to capture certain uniformities, marked by proper posture, good balance, and tension-free muscles.

Beginning with Joe Knesper, Ravielli illustrates the proper forward bend of the torso. In the larger image, Knesper is bending from the waist comfortably, with his hands dropping easily from his shoulders. In the smaller image, Ravielli illustrates a common fault: standing too far from the ball. This causes Knesper to bend too far over the ball and

2.1 Opposite: The proper amount of hip hinge allows the arms to hang straight. Standing too far from the ball causes the arms to overextend.

2.2 Opposite: Louise Suggs
shows how a golfer's build
can dictate the proper
setup. No matter the build,
a good setup allows the
golfer to make a solid,
tension-free swing.

overextend the arms. Even at this small scale, Ravielli skillfully has depicted the discomfort and tension in the body angles.(Fig. 2.1)

Next, Louise Suggs exemplifies how to adapt your stance to your build. Because we all come in different shapes and sizes, there isn't a single stance for everyone. In these three images, the principle is that a relaxed body creates the best setup.(Fig. 2.2)

Tension also can come from the arms, which should hang naturally, as Bobby Cruickshank shows in the large illustration. Lack of tension allows the swing to start smoothly and prevents faults before they happen. To check whether your arms are tension-free and hanging properly, there should be a noticeable angle between the arms and the shaft when viewed from the side. If the arms and club form a straight line, as in the smaller illustration, it means the arms are tense and not ready to start the motion.(Fig. 2.3)

The head plays a critical role in the swing, and its position at address determines whether it will help or hurt your chances of making solid contact. Patty Berg wants the head to be the swing's anchor, and Ravielli has fun with the phraseology. The second image shows how the head remains relatively centered, shifting slightly enough so the left eye can look at the back of the ball at the top of the backswing.

The third image shows a common mistake: The head has moved too far behind the ball from its original position, indicated by the highlighted circle. This indicates a sway, rather than a turn, away from the ball.(Fig. 2.4)

In addition to limiting lateral movement of the head, good players keep their chins up, literally. Many amateurs lower their chins at address, which promotes poor posture. It also limits the movement of the left shoulder and prevents a proper turn, a fault demonstrated by David Lavender on the right. Keeping the chin up gives the left shoulder room to swing under it to a full turn, as shown to the left.(Fig. 2.5)

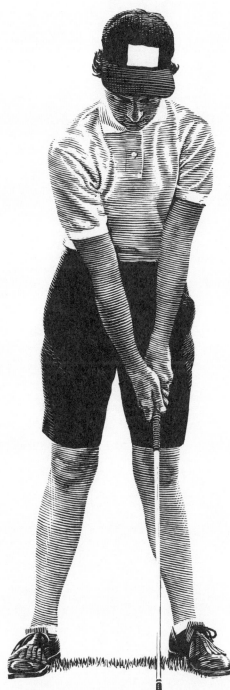

A. Ravielli

As you will learn later in this book, if you don't know already, the key to consistent golf is the path of the clubhead through impact. For all shots in which the ball is on the ground, the path should be descending through impact. With a driver and the ball on a tee, however, the path should be ascending for the best results.

Most amateurs have trouble with the driver because their path is too steep. They need to tee the ball high and hit up on the ball, which makes the image of Alex Tibbles all the more relevant with today's huge drivers. In it, he has teed the ball so almost all of it is above the clubface and has set up with the club several inches behind the ball, which encourages a sweeping motion.[(Fig. 2.6)]

There are other setup positions that promote the correct swing path. One is posture. In the smaller illustration, his stance is too wide and he is bent over too much from the waist. In the larger illustration, his stance is just right—about shoulder-width from the driver—and he is bending correctly from the waist, so his arms hang freely without tension. In addition, his head is behind the ball, which is where it should be with a driver.[(Fig. 2.7)]

In the next pair of illustrations, a straight left arm at address causes the clubhead to swing level through impact. A bent left arm promotes an out-to-in path, resulting in slices and pulls.[(Fig. 2.8)]

Finally, the two-stage illustration of Betty James shows that good setup involves more than just achieving the correct positions. Good golf, after all, is about hitting the ball toward the target, which involves getting your mind involved. James shows how to do that by staying aware of the target. Too many golfers become ball-bound and overly mechanical at address, losing track of the shot's feel and ultimate goal. Focusing on the target more will help relieve tension and free your mind of potentially harmful mechanical thoughts.[(Fig. 2.9)]

2.3 Opposite: Letting the arms hang naturally is best for a relaxed, tension-free swing. If the arms and shaft form a straight line, it is a sign of too much tension.

GOOD SETUP PROMOTES CONSISTENCY I have long held the belief that the secret to success lies in proper understanding and execution of the fundamentals. This sketch emphasizes what I believe is a vitally important—yet often overlooked—ingredient to a proper swing.

When it comes to the fundamentals, consistency is paramount. If you can repeat the same positions and moves every time, you'll simplify your technique and ingrain the correct habits. Playing good golf is similar to working on a jigsaw puzzle. The more pieces you can fit together in the beginning, the easier the rest of the puzzle will come together.

In my opinion, the width of the stance is a decision of comfort for each player. That said, as a point of reference it is wise to position your feet slightly wider than shoulder width with a driver. Then, to make the setup comfortable and the stance stable, I move my right foot closer to my left as the length of the club decreases. To promote consistency, I maintain one ball position relative to my left foot for all shots.

With short irons—8-iron through sand wedge—I make one additional adjustment, opening my stance a few degrees by pulling my left foot away from the target line about an inch. This move encourages a more out-and-up takeaway, which results in a downward attack on the ball that is necessary for solid, consistent contact. –GREG NORMAN

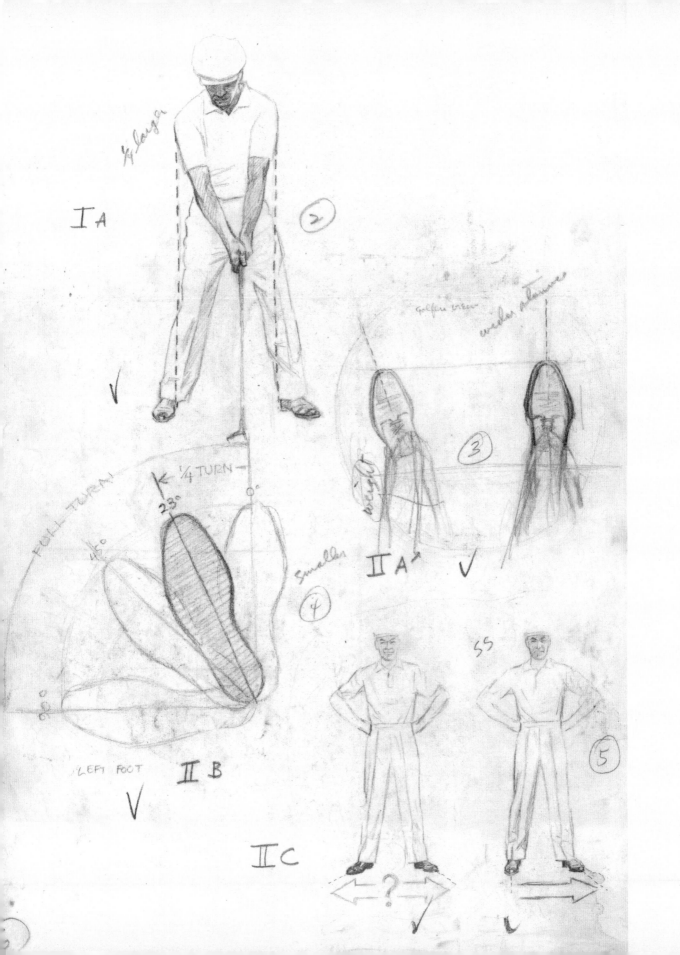

I A

½ larger

2

I A

✓

full turn

¼ TURN

45°   25°   0°

0°

smaller

4

LEFT FOOT

II B

✓

II C

golfer view   weaker stance

weight

II A'

✓

3

SS

5

?

✓

2.4 Starting at address, the body should remain centered over the ball during the swing, as if it were an anchor, as Patty Berg demonstrates.

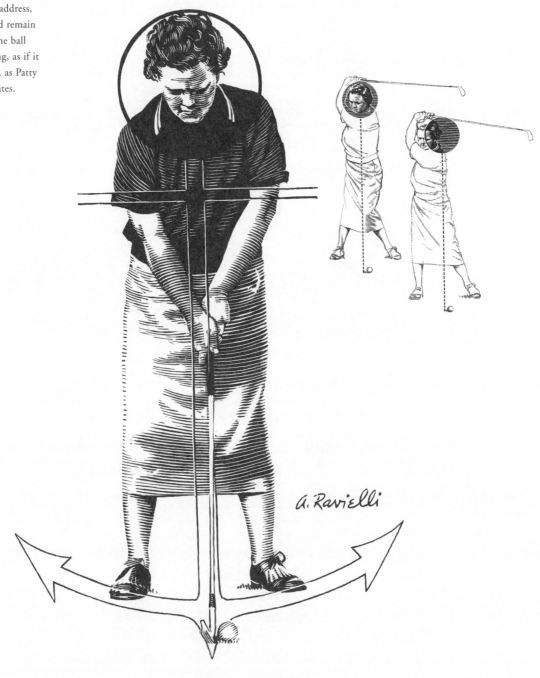

2.5 Keeping your chin
up at address will provide
enough room for the
shoulders to turn.
Burying the head will
limit shoulder turn.

PANE OF GLASS IS STILL A GREAT IMAGE Anthony Ravielli illustrated an article my father, Claude Harmon, wrote for *Sports Illustrated* in 1967, and I grew up reading Mr. Hogan's *Five Lessons*, so it was wonderful to see these drawings again.

This illustration of Mr. Hogan and the plane of glass might be the best instruction image ever created. You just glance at it and immediately understand its message: The club needs to come from the inside in the downswing.

I teach the same idea today; maybe 80 percent of the players at my golf school would shatter that plane of glass by coming over the top. The only thing old-fashioned about the drawing is how flat Mr. Hogan's plane is. Modern swings are more upright, but the idea of staying underneath the glass is still a great one.
–BUTCH HARMON

2.6 For best results with
the driver, tee the ball high
and set the club several
inches behind the ball to
promote a sweeping path
through impact.

2.7 Slouching, demon-
strated in the smaller illustration, is a common fault
that leads to a poor swing.
Better posture promotes a
more athletic swing.

A. Ravielli

2.8 Another common fault
is a bent left arm, shown on
the right. A straight left
arm promotes a better path
through impact.

a. Ravielli

2.9 Golf is an aiming game, and looking at the target often at address will help you to hit the ball at the target more often.

A. Ravielli

MUSCLES SHOW NEUTRAL SETUP Of all the incredible detail in this drawing, my favorite is the simplest: Mr. Hogan's posture and setup are neutral. His shoulders are square, and his spine is tilted slightly to the right, but not too much. His arms are hanging very naturally and relaxed—not extended with tight muscles. Even his grip is neutral—players today use stronger grips, with both hands rotated more toward the right shoulder.

His feet are set so he can unwind with maximum speed: The right foot is almost perpendicular to the target line, and the left foot is turned out, toward the target. He's in a great, athletic position—stable and ready to make a repeatable swing.
–BUTCH HARMON

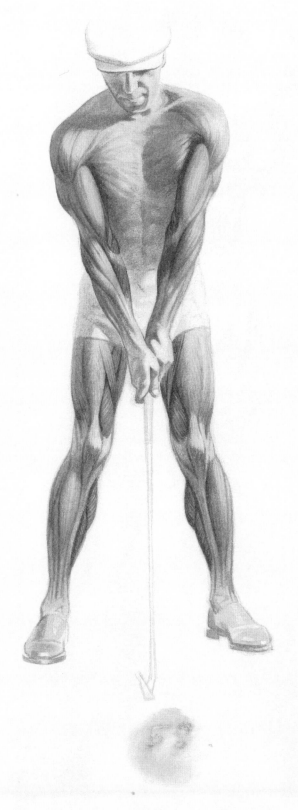

SWING | 3 | INSTRUCTION BY DAVID LEADBETTER, BILL STINES, TOM NESS, RANDY SMITH, HANK HANEY, AND MIKE McGETRICK

SWING|3| INSTRUCTION BY DAVID LEADBETTER, BILL STINES, TOM NESS, RANDY SMITH, HANK HANEY, AND MIKE McGETRICK

BACKSWING Good players make the backswing look easy. The right arm folds elegantly and simply along the body, while the upper body turns completely over a stable lower body, storing energy to be unleashed on the downswing. The club swings back naturally in concert with the chest and arms—it isn't manipulated by the hands.

The three illustrations of Peter Thomson at roughly the same point in the takeaway demonstrate the differences between the correct and incorrect. In the left drawing, Thomson has fanned the clubhead open and pulled the club too far inside with his hands at the beginning of the takeaway. In the right drawing, he has hooded the face of the club so it faces the ball, and the clubhead is too far outside. The middle drawing shows how the backswing should start, with the hands staying relatively neutral, the arms remaining in front of the chest, the club-face square, and the shaft on plane.(Fig. 3.1)

Swinging the club on the correct plane is crucial for accuracy. But what is plane, exactly? Start with the image of a player at address. You're watching him from behind the ball, looking toward the target. If you draw an imaginary line from the ball, up the shaft, and through the player's shoulders, you see Ben Hogan's famous "plane-of-glass" image. The club should go back and come down roughly along that plane for consistent results.

3.1 Opposite: In the smaller illustrations, Peter Thomson demonstrates two incorrect takeaways. On the left, the clubhead is open and the club is too far inside; on the right, the clubface is hooded and the club is too far outside. The large illustration shows a good backswing, with the clubface square and the shaft on plane.

G. Ravielli

As you can see in the Thomson drawings or the Al Mengert illustration, if a player manipulates the club with his hands, the shaft goes under or above the plane. If that happens, he must reroute the club from above or below the plane in the downswing to return to impact on plane, a move that promotes inconsistency.(Fig. 3.2)

Of course, there are exceptions—Jim Furyk won the 2003 U.S. Open with a swing that is well above the plane in the backswing, before dropping down correctly through impact. But he also hits hundreds of practice balls every day. A swing that starts on plane and stays there is easier to maintain.

The backswing is also important for generating the swing's power. Ravielli's reference photograph of Hogan's top-of-the-backswing position makes good impact seem inevitable. He couldn't help but hit the ball well from that solid, balanced position. One important lesson from that photograph is the concept of coil—Hogan's shoulders have turned away from the ball far more than his hips have.(Fig. 3.4)

Coil is what stores power in the backswing, so it can be unleashed in the downswing. The more difference you can have between the shoulder and hip turn, the greater the coil.

Some players try to get more power by making what they think is a big turn away from the ball. But if the hips and shoulders turn away from the ball to the same degree, as they do in the small image of Jimmy Hines, you aren't achieving coil. The same is true if you slide your body away from the target instead of turning the shoulders. Too much lateral motion robs your swing of the leverage and speed created by the sequential uncoiling of the hips, shoulders, and arms.(Fig. 3.3)

When performed correctly, the position at the top of the backswing should be similar to holding a tray with the right hand over the right shoulder.(Fig. 3.5)

3.2 Opposite: An incorrect swing plane, whether above or below, requires the player to re-route the club in the downswing, a move that promotes inconsistency.

3.3 BACKSWING CREATES COIL Don't worry about the position of the club to determine the correct backswing length. It can be misleading. In the left drawing, Jimmy Hines makes a complete turn, although the shaft is nowhere near parallel. His left shoulder has turned under his chin and is inside the left hip pocket, indicating the proper 90-degree turn, and his left hip has turned level into the right side to about 45 degrees—again, ideal.

The shoulders should always make the biggest turn in the backswing, and you should feel some tension and resistance in the muscles of your left side at the top of the backswing. This sets up the downswing, which begins with the unwinding of the hips, followed by the shoulder as they release the speed and power built up by the coil and resistance in the backswing.

Even though the shaft has reached parallel in the drawing to the right, this is an improper turn. There is too much rotation in both the shoulders and the hips, which means there is lack of resistance in the left side. This backswing is a major power leak, and he will be trying to create speed with his hands and arms, which are less effective than the big muscles of the legs and torso.
–BILL STINES

TRANSITION

When players and teachers talk about "tempo," they're really talking about the transition between the backswing and the downswing. Players with great tempo, like Ernie Els or Retief Goosen, look effortless because they make a smooth, controlled transition without any jerky acceleration.

In the backswing, a player is trying to store up as much potential energy as possible. One of the Ben Hogan photographs Anthony Ravielli used as a reference for his drawings perfectly captures this idea of controlled, coiled energy. Then, in a good downswing, the body unwinds in the correct sequence, causing the clubhead to speed up gradually until it reaches maximum speed through impact.

The Wally Grant drawings show how the hips—not the clubhead—initiate the transition. Grant's hips start turning back toward the target, his left foot plants, and the shoulders follow the hips' lead. The hands and clubhead lag behind before cracking through impact powerfully, like the tip of a whip. (Fig. 3.6)

A sign of bad transition is the application of the swing's power at the wrong time. If a player is too quick and starts the downswing before making a full, complete backswing, the hands and clubhead fire too soon, out of sequence. This wastes the swing's stored energy before the clubhead reaches the ball.

Good players often suffer from the opposite problem. In an effort to turn the hips faster in the downswing, the upper body lags behind, and the arms get "stuck"—a term popularized by Tiger Woods—behind the body instead of swinging properly in front of it. From that position, the only possible recovery is to throw the clubhead toward the ball with the hands, a recipe for inconsistency and a major reason Woods found so few fairways in 2004.

A less thought about but no less important area of transition is the

3.5 At the top of the
backswing, you should feel
as if you are holding a tray
with your right hand.

3.6 DOWNSWING STARTS WITH "SQUAT" Wally Grant is demonstrating a good transition from the backswing to the downswing. The pivoting body drags the club downward and outward toward impact—and from the ground up, not from the club first. The left foot goes from rolled on the instep at the top to flat on the ground, and the space between the knees widens as the hips begin to open. That will give him the classic "squat" that Hogan made so famous. –TOM NESS

A. Ravielli

3.7 Opposite: Steel shafts become popular in the 1950's, doing away with the need for a smooth transition from address to the takeaway shown at right. The modern one-piece takeaway is shown at left.

beginning of the swing, in which rhythm and tempo are crucial for setting the right tone for the rest of the swing. As indicated in the previous chapters on grip and setup, lack of tension promotes good tempo.

If you have trouble with tempo, just be glad you didn't learn to play in the hickory-shaft era, which ended in the 1930s. Hickory was so flexible that any active wrist cocking at the beginning of the swing caused it to flex out of control. Players had to drag the club slowly away from the ball with the clubhead trailing behind the hands. Tempo was very important in those days, causing Bobby Jones to observe famously, "Nobody every swung a club too slowly."

For a generation of hickory-shaft users, this drag takeaway lasted well into the 1950s, which is when Ravielli made this drawing of Danny Lavender. When steel shafts came into widespread use, the modern turn-and-wrist-cock backswing shown in the left illustration became the standard.[Fig. 3.7]

A. Ravielli

DECREASE ANGLE TO CURE CASTING Casting the club from the top is the cancer of the average player's golf swing. Casting, or throwing the club from the top, is a major power leak that also robs accuracy. This picture shows how to prevent casting. The angle created by Frank Stranahan's arms and shaft decreases as he moves into his downswing—from the lightly shaded club to the bolder one.

This down-cocking move is the best defense against casting, in which the angle actually increases. To make a good transition like this, you have to have constant, light grip pressure. The moment your grip gets too tight, you'll throw the club from the top.
–TOM NESS

SYNCHRONIZE BODY WITH ARMS This is an ideal top-of-the-backswing position. The arms are in front of a fully coiled body. The arms should remain synchronized with the body all the way through the downswing—and not race ahead, in an effort to hit at the ball.

The small picture shows what happens when the body races ahead, trapping the arms behind it. This happens frequently to players who are concentrating on the body—trying to clear the hips or something similar. The player who struggles with this often tries to fix it by throwing the clubhead at the ball. That's not a fix but a case of a flaw creating another flaw. To fix both problems, concentrate on driving the hands at the ball. The body will pivot naturally, as if you were tossing a ball down the fairway.
–TOM NESS

3.8 BOBBY JONES'S FIRST MOVE DOWN Mr. Jones is demonstrating incredible hip turn in his backswing. Look how far his left heel has come off the ground to accommodate it. With improvements in equipment—stiffer, more consistent shafts, for one—this kind of hip turn is no longer necessary in the modern swing, but players should still turn their shoulders the way Mr. Jones did. Look how his shoulders coil as the hips unwind into the left side. You also see the left foot replanting to support the shift into the left side. This part of the swing is textbook, even for the great swings of today. –RANDY SMITH

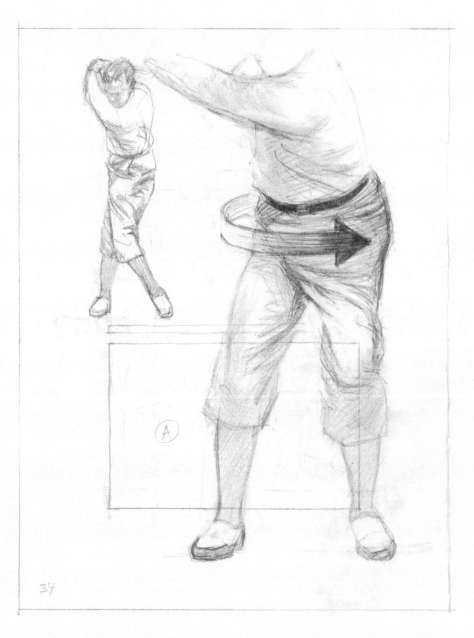

DOWNSWING In the downswing a player is applying the energy stored during the backswing coil. After a smooth transition between the backswing and downswing, the lower body leads, the upper body follows, and the hands and club trail. A good downswing almost should be a chain reaction, free of any conscious action. The sketch of Bobby Jones's hip turn[Fig. 3.8] and Jackie Pung's shadow illustrations[Fig. 3.9] show how the lower body initiates this chain reaction.

The two most common problems average players have with their downswings are path and sequencing. Along with an open clubface at impact, a player hits a slice because his or her swing path cuts across the ball from the outside to the inside. Most good players' swing paths go from inside to outside.

The second problem, sequencing, is usually related to the first. The downswing should unwind from the ground up. If the arms or hands move out of sequence—usually in an effort to hit at the ball—the sequencing of the downswing is destroyed, and the player can't hit the ball far or straight.

In the "over-the-top" move, the player starts his or her downswing with the arms and hands instead of the lower body, and the club immediately moves outside the correct path. As the player turns through impact, the club cuts back across the ball, causing either a weak slice or a pull.

In addition to creating an out-to-in path, manipulating the club with the arms in an effort to produce more distance actually does the opposite and slows down the club because there is too much tension in the arms and hands. Tight, restricted muscles are the opposite of what you want. Instead, let centrifugal force accelerate the clubhead and produce long, straight shots.

The ultimate goal of the downswing is consistent impact, and ball

A. Ravielli

position also makes a big difference. With an iron, the ball should correspond with the point just before the low point of the downswing. In other words, the club should be descending at impact, before hitting the ground and taking a divot before it starts up again toward the finish.

Off a tee with a driver, ball position should be more forward, toward the target, allowing the bottom of the downswing to come just before impact, so the clubhead is ascending slightly as it meets the ball. An otherwise solid downswing can be ruined with a bad setup or a mistake in ball position. If the swing bottoms out in the wrong place in relation to the ball, the result is usually less than pretty—fat shots, thin shots, skulls, or chili-dips.

3.9 Opposite: Through the use of her shadow, Jackie Pung shows how the lower body initiates the downswing, so the hands and club lag behind.

DOWNSWING IS LIKE A BASEBALL SWING In both the baseball and golf swing, a strong weight shift to the front leg sets up a powerful impact position, as well as an inside path for the bat or club to attack the ball. Both positions show how the front knee should be outside the left shoulder on the downswing to promote that strong, athletic impact position.

The main difference is that the baseball player has opened his upper body more than the golfer to accommodate the horizontal swing path. –RANDY SMITH

BURY RIGHT ELBOW INTO SIDE This position is right out of
the Paul Bertholy book on the golf swing, and it shows the right
elbow's very important role in delaying the release of the hands in
the downswing. The right elbow buries into the right side to create
lag, which produces tremendous power. This is a marvelous
illustration of a powerful swing, but if you make this move, you
have to be sure to rotate the lower body aggressively into and
through impact. –RANDY SMITH

A. Ravielli

IMPACT The goal of any swing is to produce a solid, square impact position, and all the drawings and instructor tips in this book are designed to help reach this position every time.

Most teachers start a first lesson by watching the student hit balls. The teacher is watching impact—what the ball does when it comes off the club—and it doesn't lie. A player who comes over the top will make a glancing blow across the ball from outside to in, which produces a high, weak shot to the right. Other swing problems lead to poor impact positions that cause fat or thin shots, pulls or hooks. The teacher then comes up with a plan to improve the chain reaction that leads to the swing's moment of truth: impact.

To improve impact, it helps first to understand how a great impact position feels: the clubhead making a descending blow so it hits the ball first then the turf (with an iron), and the left arm and shaft in a straight line. Once a player feels that sensation of perfectly unleashed power and accuracy several times, he or she receives a frame of reference for the swing improvements that have to be made and finally can recognize those eureka moments when the ball flies straight and long.

Ravielli was one of the few artists with the talent to capture the energy and force of the impact position in such a dynamic way—in a two-dimensional medium. The drawing of Hogan at impact, from *Five Lessons*, looks like a still frame from a video. The amazing details of the muscles of the arms and the folds in the pant legs subtly add to the feeling of motion.(Fig. 3.10)

Whether in Hogan's timeless position or Tom Watson's wonderful postimpact extension,(Fig. 3.11) Ravielli's drawings have the unique ability to communicate the feel of solid impact. That extra dimension separated Ravielli's work from the rest, and it is one of the main reasons Hogan and Bobby Jones, among others, trusted Ravielli so completely to re-create their swings for instruction books.

3.10 HOGAN'S PERFECT IMPACT Ben Hogan's classic impact position is the model everyone should try to imitate. The back of Mr. Hogan's left hand is facing the target and so is the clubface, an indication of a neutral grip. The left arm and club form a straight line, the most powerful impact position. Additionally, the left hand is not only square but turned down slightly, a key for making solid ball-turf contact.

As for the body, Mr. Hogan's hips have not only turned through, they also have shifted to the left so his weight is primarily on his left side at impact. In addition, his right foot rolls in while the heel rises just slightly—a key to keeping posture coming into impact. These positions really show why Mr. Hogan was the ultimate ball-striker. –HANK HANEY

G. Ravielli

3.11 WATSON'S IMPACT PROMOTES A DRAW Tom Watson's position just after impact shows that his shot will have a slight draw, from right to left. The club has come into the ball from inside and on an arc that goes slightly to the right of the target line after impact, before it swings around his body and to the left. His hips have led the downswing—they have turned more to the left than his shoulders at this point in his swing. Although Watson's hips are leading, his head has stayed back and his right heel hasn't lifted off the ground too much for this point in his swing—two keys to coming into the ball from the inside path. –HANK HANEY

FINISH The finish says a lot about the golf swing that came before it. Arnold Palmer's unorthodox twist at the end of his follow-through was a continuation of his forceful, workmanlike slash through impact. Ernie Els's finish position is as graceful and balanced as his easy action. Although these finishes are different, they both show a player in control of his swing. Both players turn their hips completely through impact, so the belt buckle points left of the target. Almost all their weight has moved to the outside of the left foot—meaning it has transferred through the shot instead of hanging back.

When the swing and finish are performed correctly, the swing's arc should come from inside the target line in the downswing, travel along the target line at address, and move back inside the line in the follow-through, as Ravielli deftly demonstrates in an overhead view. Often, amateurs have an incorrect idea of what the correct swing path should look like. The solid line represents the clubhead's path. When done correctly, the ball should travel straight, as indicated by the dotted line.[Fig. 3.12]

Why do teachers spend so much time on the finish, when the so-called "important" part of the swing, impact, is done? Because the only way a player can get into Tom Watson's beautiful, fully extended position in the follow-through is to make the correct moves earlier in the swing.[Fig. 3.13]

The same is true for the other drawing of Watson in his finish position. This fully turned, relaxed, and balanced pose is the result of a chain reaction of good fundamentals, starting at address.[Fig. 3.14] When the average player gets tied up in swing thoughts and ideas about technique, teachers can often circumvent the problem by getting him or her to simply think about the Watson finish position. Instead of thinking about a disjointed series of positions, the player starts thinking of the swing as a fluid motion with the finish as the end goal, and those positions start to blend smoothly.

3.12 This overhead view
shows the correct arc of the
clubhead—from the inside
in the downswing, straight
down the target line at
impact, then back inside in
the follow-through.

3.13 Tom Watson's
extended finish position is
only possible through
correct movements earlier
in the swing.

a. Ravielli

3.14 In a good finish, a
player should be able to
hold the pose for several
seconds, as Watson is
doing here.

HOW TO READ THE FINISH What can you learn from a good finish? Good swings start in balance and finish in balance, so just learning to finish in a balanced position will help your overall swing. Mike Souchak's finish is one I'd teach today. He has turned left of his target, and the majority of his weight is on the front leg, as indicated by the slight roll to the outside of the left foot.

Another good characteristic is a slight reverse C—the back is arched a bit so the head is slightly farther from the target than the belt buckle. This position shows that the club came down on the right path in the forward swing.

In the smaller picture, a lot of weight remains on the back foot, a common problem among amateurs. That usually is the result of trying to over-accelerate from the top and hit at the ball. The hips spin out, forcing the left foot to open up like this, and you waste all your power. Starting the forward swing should be a gradual acceleration. Build up the speed through impact instead of thinking in terms of fast starts or stops. When done correctly, you should be able to lift your right foot off the ground from your finish position. –MIKE McGETRICK

A SWING BROUGHT TO LIFE One of the things I admire most about Ben Hogan's swing—its beautiful sequencing—comes through with incredible detail in these drawings. In the backswing, the arms move away, then the body winds up. You can see a definite relationship between the arm swing and body turn. The third picture gives a great sense of coil—right down to the wrinkles on his shirt and pant legs.

The fourth drawing is what I would call relaxed coil. The body is fully wound up, but the arms almost look soft, providing the sense that the arms are swinging, not tense and tight. The players who can make this relaxed coil—Mr. Hogan, or Ernie Els today—make the swing look so easy. It's the epitome of effortless power. It's a majestic sight—the swing looks simple and smooth, but the club just fizzes through impact.

What's amazing about these drawings is the way they are able to capture that fluidity. You move your eyes back and forth seamlessly from the first drawing to the last, giving the impression that Mr. Hogan's swing is in motion, right on the page. It's almost as if you're watching a swing on film. –DAVID LEADBETTER

IRONS | 4 |

INSTRUCTION
BY
DR. JIM SUTTIE

IRONS |4|

INSTRUCTION
BY
DR. JIM SUTTIE

BROWSING THROUGH THE COLLECTION of iron-play drawings collected here is like finding a fossilized television remote control at an archaeological dig in Egypt. Plenty in golf has changed since 1950, but average golfers are struggling with many of the same problems—slicing, coming over the top, inconsistency. The physics of the golf swing haven't changed, which gives these drawings a timeless quality.

There's something reassuring, and a little discouraging, about that realization. It shows we're working on the right problems: Today's golfer could just as easily learn and improve from these drawings as a player who originally saw them 50 years ago. However, it also means those faults are remarkably persistent and not so easy to fix, even with revolutionary developments in iron technology, like perimeter weighting and ultralight graphite shafts.

The most exciting drawings in this collection are the full-body sequence studies, the backbone of *Golf Digest*'s instruction coverage, then and now. They give us the most complete two-dimensional view of some of the most famous swings of the era, from Tommy Bolt to Ben Hogan.

The three-panel illustration of Bolt's swing works in a similar way to the high-speed photographic swing sequences that *Golf Digest* publishes today. The drawings show how Bolt's weight shifts from his right foot to his left, and how the clubhead releases through impact. One interesting note is how his legs move. Bolt's knees separate through impact, then close again at the finish. This shows that Bolt is turning through impact, not sliding his hips down the target line.(Fig. 4.1)

The next drawing, of Jim Turnesa, is a similar pre- and postimpact study, but the different angles show how the shoulders work in the swing. Going back, Turnesa turns his left shoulder until it is under his chin. Then, he moves his right shoulder down and through on the downswing, until it is under his chin at the finish.(Fig. 4.2)

Some of the drawings reproduced here should be easily recognizable, at least in terms of content, to anyone who reads modern golf magazines. Teachers are still trying to get students to do what Wiffi Smith is demonstrating in her tip: Trust the loft of the club to get the ball airborne and avoid scooping the shot into the air with the hands and wrists.(Fig. 4.3) Jay Hebert's tip illustrates the same point. Instead of letting the right hand overpower the left, which has broken down, the good player's hands perform in the opposite way: The left wrist is actually bowed while the right wrist is bent at impact. In other words, the club actually should have less loft at impact than it did at address—not more, as it would if you tried to scoop.(Fig. 4.4)

This is just as true with long irons as it is with wedges. The last two drawings are classics: Turnesa's tip gives timeless advice about setting up with the ball in the center of the clubhead, not toward the toe or heel.(Fig. 4.5) Stan Leonard demonstrates the subtle differences between a full swing and a three-quarter shot—a bit more shoulder turn and wrist cock for the full shot than for the shorter shot. Other than that, everything else is the same, which makes it easier to make solid contact.(Fig. 4.6)

Ravielli was really able to show off his artistic skill in drawings like

A. Ravielli

4.1 A WEIGHT SHIFT TO EMULATE Tommy Bolt is showing complete extension and width at impact and into the follow-through. This was a result of the wonderful use of his lower body on the downswing—his footwork and lower-body shift to the left side were second to none. Also, notice his flat left wrist at impact, and how the butt of the club is pointing to the center of his body. These positions indicate a complete and neutral release.

Bolt was one of the first of the "body" players. He could hit the ball hard with his hands because he had such great movement with his lower body. All amateurs, particularly the chicken-wingers, should try to copy his great release and the connection of his upper left arm to his body. –DR. JIM SUTTIE

A. Ravielli

4.3 Wiffi Smith trusts the
loft of the club to get
the ball airborne, instead of
trying to scoop the ball
into the air with her hands
and wrists.

A. Ravielli

the Leonard example. It took a considerable understanding of physics, physiology, and the mechanics of the swing to show the slight variations between the two swings in a way that the average reader could understand immediately. Ravielli accomplished that with shading methods—fully shaded drawings depicted a finished or good position, while lighter shadings represented preliminary steps or poor positions.

Another staple of monthly magazine instruction through the decades is the two-panel tip showing right and wrong swing positions. One of the hardest things for good players to do is show a bad position, simply because they don't know how. But Ravielli somehow coaxed the pros into mimicking the high handicappers they were trying to help.

Dow Finsterwald's lesson shows the difference between making a fake turn with just the arms and a real turn with the hips and shoulders in the backswing. The left knee moves in dramatically different ways in each swing—down toward the ball in the poor example, and back toward the right knee in the good one.[(Fig. 4.7)]

In each example, Ravielli's skill provides a clear roadmap for avoiding the fault and achieving the fix.

4.4 Opposite: In a good iron swing, the left wrist actually should bow at impact, delofting the club instead of adding loft.

4.5 Setting up with the ball centered on the clubface will yield the most consistent results.

A. Ravielli

4.6 Stan Leonard demon-
strates that for partial shots,
the only adjustment is
the length of the swing;
nothing else changes.

A. Ravielli

4.7 Often the sign of a
good weight shift is where
the left knee points. In a
good turn, it points behind
the ball; in a bad swing,
as the small illustration
shows, the left knee points
in front of the ball.

G. Ravielli

WOODS |5| INSTRUCTION BY RICK SMITH AND JIM FLICK

5.1 NELSON'S IDEAL BACKSWING This is just a wonderful depiction of the halfway point of the backswing. Byron Nelson's spine angle has remained intact from address, and his hands are still in front of his chest. There's a little bit of a turn happening, but the hands haven't moved up or behind the chest, and the club hasn't fanned open—all common faults. Notice also that the elbows are the same distance apart as they probably were at address. Lastly, the handle is still pointing to the ball, indicating ideal swing plane.

To sum up, Mr. Nelson's backswing shows good spine angle, no hand manipulation, and good plane: these are all absolute critical elements of a good golf swing, and it's easy to see why he won 11 consecutive tournaments in 1945. –RICK SMITH

WOODS |5| INSTRUCTION BY RICK SMITH AND JIM FLICK

NO PART OF THE GAME HAS CHANGED more in the last 50 years than wood play. New clubhead materials, lighter, more consistent shafts, and stronger, more athletic players have transformed the long game and rendered an entire genre of classic golf courses—6,000-yard parkland layouts—virtually obsolete for pros and top amateurs.

Champions Tour players who never reached par 5s in two shots during their regular tour heydays routinely putt for eagle now. Big hitters like Ernie Els and Tiger Woods hit mid-irons into 590-yard par 5s. Even a hacker with reasonable clubhead speed can expect to hit at least one drive per round in the 280-yard range.

Does this mean the dozens of Anthony Ravielli's drawings on the driver and fairway woods are obsolete? Yes and no. Byron Nelson's gorgeous backswing position is effortless, a timeless reminder for all giant-clubhead-swinging amateurs who make out-of-control lunges at the ball.[Fig. 5.1] Likewise, Bobby Cruickshank's advice about lowering the right shoulder slightly at address is just as helpful with today's titanium drivers as it was in 1950 with a persimmon club in hand.[Fig. 5.2]

In Ravielli's time, the driver and fairway woods were the least forgiving clubs in the bag because of their size, or lack thereof: The average persimmon driver's volume was 165 cubic centimeters, while

5.2 DON'T NEGLECT SHOULDER ALIGNMENT These

drawings really show how to check your shoulder alignment, a major indicator of swing path and proper turn. You have to make sure that your shoulders are parallel to the target line. People get so caught up about where their feet line up that they forget to check the shoulders.

In the bigger illustration, notice the slight spine tilt away from the target. This is important for good driving because it makes it easier to turn without moving off the ball too much, and it also lets you make an ascending blow, which is important for the driver. I really like the grip in this drawing, too. The "V"s are parallel to each other, and they're inside the right shoulder and right ear. You'll get good speed this way, with no manipulative hand action. –RICK SMITH

today's drivers max out at 460cc. As a result, their sweet spots were tiny, requiring near-perfect contact to produce good shots. The instruction of the day touched on many of the same issues you read about today in *Golf Digest*—sequencing the body, swing plane, and retaining posture from address through impact—but with an even greater emphasis on consistency and accuracy, rather than distance.

Most accuracy faults take place during setup, so many of Ravielli's drawings depict what should happen before the start of the swing. Gene Sarazen, who hit the greatest wood shot in golf history, his 4-wood for double eagle on the 15th hole during the final round of the 1935 Masters, shows how to set up squarely for a wood shot. Notice how his feet, legs, and arms are lined up squarely.[Fig. 5.3]

Sarazen also demonstrates why it is so difficult to hit a driver from the fairway. In the top close-up of the fairway wood, the top of the ball is above the top of the club, allowing the club to make contact below the ball's center of gravity, sending the shot soaring. Below, the face of the driver is higher than the top of the ball, which means impact will be made above the ball's center of gravity. The effect is even greater with today's supersize drivers; only players with extremely high club-head speed should try to hit a driver from the fairway.

Frank Stranahan shows how to prevent incorrect alignment by approaching the ball from behind it.[Fig. 5.4] Many recreational players have a grip that is too weak, which causes a slice. Kathy Cornelius wants the "V" created by the thumb and the side of the left hand to point toward the right shoulder, a stronger position that promotes a draw, and not straight up the shaft.[Fig. 5.5]

However, sometimes it is necessary to hit an intentional left-to-right shot, like when you really have to hit the fairway—a fade is easier to control. To do so, Buck Luce demonstrates how the grip has to be

5.3 Gene Sarazen demonstrates how the ball is higher than the face of a fairway wood, allowing the club to make contact below the equator of the ball and promoting a higher launch and longer carry. Below, the deep face of the driver makes it harder to hit off the fairway.

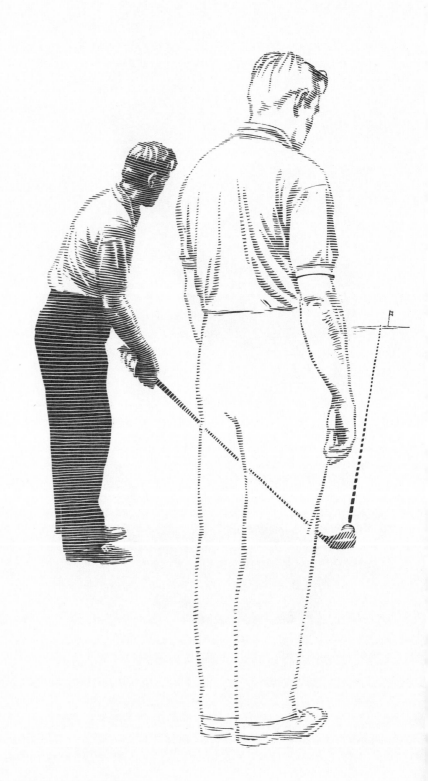

5.4 Frank Stranahan shows
how to aim properly by
approaching the ball from
behind it.

A. Ravielli

5.5 A strong grip, in which the "V" created by the left thumb and hand points to the right shoulder, is often best for amateurs.

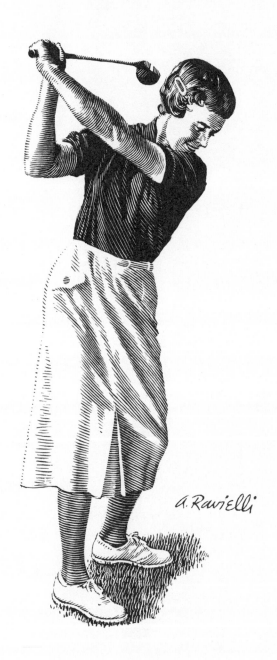

a. Ravielli

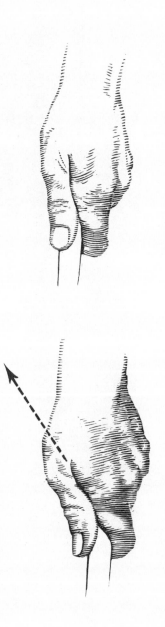

5.6 When finding the fairway is a must, a weaker grip is best for hitting a controlled fade.

a. Ravielli

5.7 A waggle helps keep
tension out of the swing.

5.8 Even in a sport coat,
the arms are relaxed and
ready to begin the swing.

[WOODS]

5.9 For proper alignment, set up clubface first, then set the feet in line with the club.

A. Ravielli

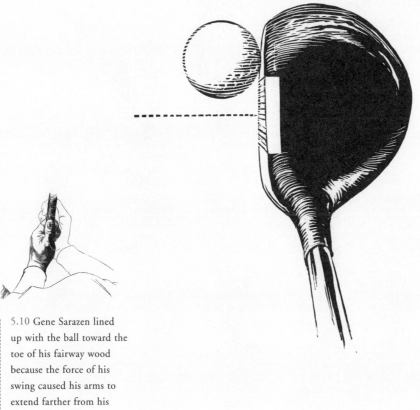

5.10 Gene Sarazen lined up with the ball toward the toe of his fairway wood because the force of his swing caused his arms to extend farther from his body at impact.

5.11 Mike Turnesa's address
position, with perfect balance, good spine angle, and
excellent posture, is ideal.

5.12 Lionel Hebert is
building power in his
backswing. Notice the
wrinkles in his pants,
indicating a weight shift
into his right side.

weaker, with the V pointing up the grip, which Ravielli shows from the golfer's point of view.(Fig. 5.6) The drawing of Jim Fogarty illustrates the process of waggling the club at address to keep tension out of the hands and forearms.(Fig. 5.7)

Four address drawings, two of anonymous players and the other two of Mike Turnesa and Gene Sarazen, show the wood setup from various angles. Sport coat and tie notwithstanding, the first drawing is notable for how relaxed the arms and legs look.(Fig. 5.8) The second address drawing illustrates the proper sequence in which to set up to the ball, by lining up the clubface first before taking the stance.(Fig. 5.9) Sarazen is showing how he set up with the ball lined up toward the toe of his fairway wood because the force of his downswing caused his arms to extend farther from the body at impact.(Fig. 5.10) The up-the-line view of Turnesa's setup with a fairway wood shows the same sense of relaxed preparedness, as well as perfect balance, with ideal spine angle and chin held high. Players from any era should copy this position.(Fig. 5.11)

The illustration of Lionel Hebert shows the start of the backswing. Ravielli has captured the folds in Hebert's left pant leg, showing that his weight is moving from that leg to the braced right leg. Hebert's clubface is slightly closed—modern players try to keep the face vertical at this point in the swing—but his arms are in good position, still in front of his chest and somewhat soft, not overextended.(Fig. 5.12)

Although the angle is different, the Stan Leonard drawing shows the stage of the backswing following Hebert's position. As Leonard's weight loads almost fully onto the right side, the left heel has come slightly off the ground and the left knee is fully flexed. You can even see the stretch creases in the back of his shirt, indicating the proper coil of his upper body over a stable lower body.(Fig. 5.13)

Ravielli's drawings of Ben Hogan in the groundbreaking *Five Lessons*

5.13 Opposite: Stan Leonard's weight is shifting fully onto his right side as he completes his backswing, a powerful position.

A. Ravielli

WIDE ARC GREAT FOR WOOD SHOTS

The swing on the left has a wide arc, without too much tension. The left heel coming off the ground is great for the less supple player to emulate, because it makes it much easier to turn. A lot of players try to keep the head down during the backswing, but they don't have the flexibility to do that. It usually causes a reverse pivot, which leads to the weight shifting the wrong way—away from the target—in the downswing.

I like the drawing on the left for some other reasons. The left wrist is slightly cupped at the top, like Jack Nicklaus, Ben Hogan, or Vijay Singh. This means the clubface is square to open, which promotes a releasing of the forearms through impact.

This drawing on the right shows numerous faults. The right knee has straightened and is locked. This kind of tension creates tight, slow muscles with no feel. Also, see how much higher his right hip is than the left? Not good—in this position, the lower body is unstable, leading to too much inconsistency. The clubface is also open, which will make it difficult to square the clubface at impact. –JIM FLICK

5.14 Notice how Harry
Obitz's right elbow
has returned to his side,
a powerful move.

A. Ravielli

5.15 The smaller illustration is a weak position, with the club approaching the ball from outside the line. The bigger image indicates the proper path, from slightly inside the line.

A. Ravielli

A SLICE CURE This drawing is obviously geared toward a slicer, who senses a shot going to the left and makes this move in the smaller picture with the left elbow, which keeps the face from closing and sends the ball to the right. However, the "chicken wing" creates a very weak impact position.

The larger, improved example shows better forearm rotation—knuckles down through impact instead of up. The right forearm looks like it's rotating to the left, as is the left. In addition, the left elbow is much softer and closer to the body instead of pointing out. –RICK SMITH

familiarized a generation of players with Hogan's classic downswing squat—the separation of his knees as his right elbow returned to his side. Two drawings show variations of that "Hogan squat." Harry Obitz is in what he called the "classic position"—the left hand pulling the club while the club is returning to the ball from inside the target line.[Fig. 5.14]

By contrast, many poor players are in the position Bill Wortherspoon is demonstrating. In the small illustration, he is coming over the top and swinging the club from outside the target line, which causes slices and pulls. On the left, he's making the correct move, which is similar to Obitz's position. You can see how Wortherspoon's hips have already turned past the ball, allowing the left hand to pull the club through impact.[Fig. 5.15]

The following three drawings vividly show what happens next during a wood swing. Through impact, Jay Hebert's hips have turned more than his shoulders, almost all of his weight has shifted to his left foot, and his arms have extended well past the ball.[Fig. 5.16] From a face-on angle, the next drawing shows the same arm extension in the follow-through, as well as a full unwinding of the upper body and the weight shift—see how the right heel has come off the ground.[Fig. 5.17] Finally, by unwinding fully and getting over to the left foot, Wiffi Smith is able to hold her balanced finish indefinitely, as if she were posing for Ravielli.[Fig. 5.18] Being able to hold your finish is the sign of a smooth, balanced swing and is something you should try to do on every full shot.

5.17 A full release is often
accompanied by a
powerful weight shift.
Notice how the right heel
is off the ground.

A. Ravielli

5.18 A complete, balanced finish is a sign of a long, straight shot.

A. Ravielli

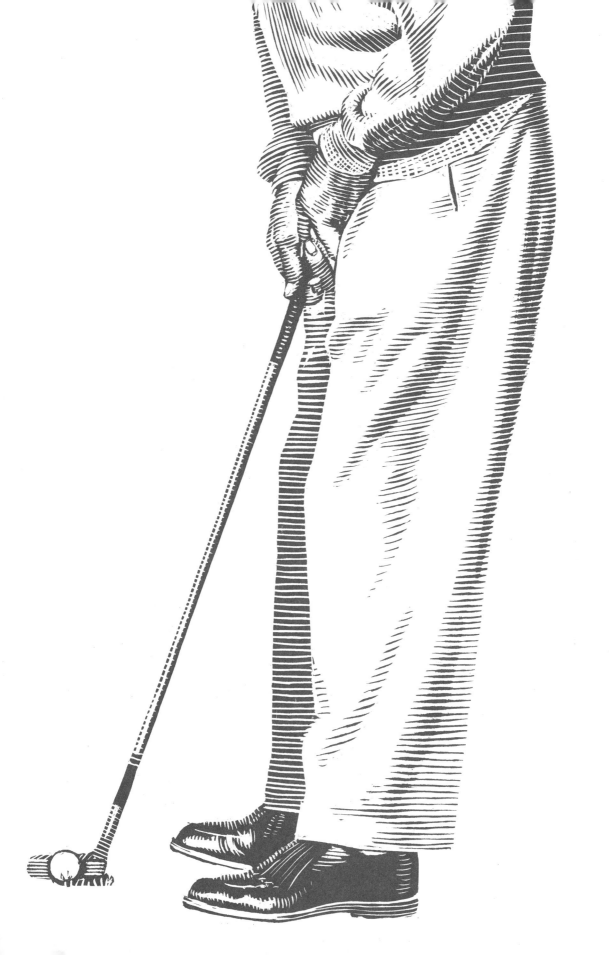

PUTTING | 6 | INSTRUCTION BY STAN UTLEY

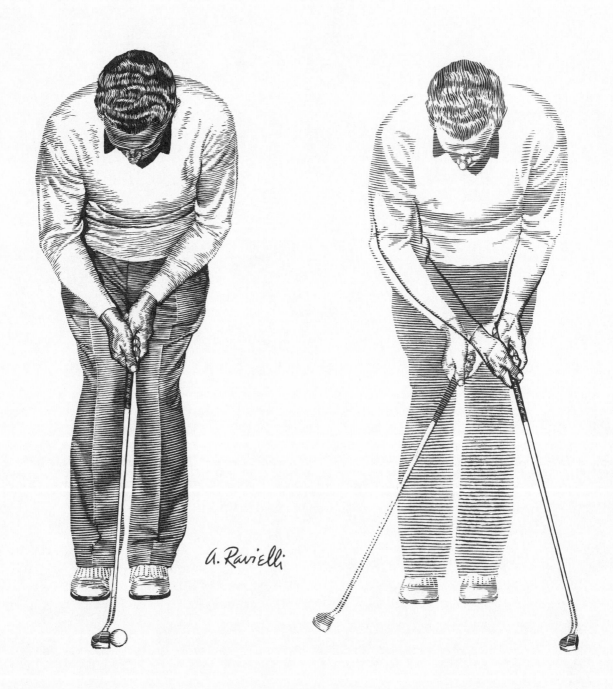

A. Ravielli

PUTTING |6|

INSTRUCTION
BY
STAN UTLEY

IN NO OTHER SECTION of this book—or in golf instruction in general—will you find such a wide range of accepted styles. If the golf swing can be boiled down to the elegant simplicity of physics in motion, putting can be described as art, as subject as a blank canvas to the interpretation and inspiration of its creator. The great champions of the last 100 years had certain qualities in common, like the ability to make the big putt when it was absolutely necessary, but they didn't share common putting mechanics.

Bobby Jones won 13 major championships with an upright, narrow stance, and sweeping stroke, while Arnold Palmer crouched over his putts like a man trying to make his way through a chicken-wire fence and made a fast, short, piston-like jab.

Paging through Anthony Ravielli's collection of instruction drawings about putting demonstrates this individuality. The methods Ravielli faithfully reproduced for *Golf Digest* ranged from the unorthodox, like Al Besselink's wrists-only stroke,[(Fig. 6.1)] to the conventional, like JoAnn Prentice's demonstration of a good putting grip.[(Fig. 6.2)]

Variety exists even in today's putting strokes. Some professionals subscribe to the idea that the putter should move straight back and through along an imaginary line through the ball, in a pendulum

6.1 Opposite: Al Besselink shows a wristy stroke, which has fallen out of favor among today's top golfers.

6.2 Comfort is key for a
relaxed putting stroke.

6.3 Tension is the enemy of good putting; even from the fringe, Billy Maxwell demonstrates a light touch.

a. Ravielli

6.4 A square, neutral grip,
as demonstrated by Ralph
Hutchinson, is often best
for good putting.

LET YOUR INSTINCT COME OUT This is a great image. He's showing the importance of athleticism and instinct in putting. I encourage a putting motion that allows the player's natural talent and feel to come out. That can't happen if you're worrying too much about mechanics. That's not to say technique isn't involved; just don't let it make your stroke rigid or stiff. —STAN UTLEY

6.5 Opposite:
Horton Smith has built
a stable platform that
allows his arms and
shoulders to control the
putting stroke.

motion. Other players think of the putting stroke as a mini-swing, and move the putter on an arc. Phil Mickelson won the Masters last year with the help of putting guru Dave Pelz, who teaches the pendulum technique. Darren Clarke and Jay Haas are among a group of players working with Stan Utley, a *Golf Digest* contributor who teaches the arc stroke and comments on several drawings in this chapter.

No matter which method you use, the key to good putting is ultimately about having confidence in your stroke and being able to repeat it under pressure. The methods are just ways to make it easier to achieve those goals, and whichever you choose is a matter of personal preference.

Of course, there are some fundamentals common to all great putters. One of the most important is good touch, which comes from lack of tension in the hands. Ravielli's style is particularly adept at recreating the delicate intricacies of the grip, especially the sense of lightness in pressure that photographs have a difficult time capturing. The best example of this looseness is the drawing of Billy Maxwell for a tip on putting from the fringe.[Fig. 6.3] Maxwell's hands look completely relaxed, as do Ralph Hutchinson's in his demonstration of the basics of the reverse overlap grip.[Fig. 6.4]

The following drawings from this period follow some common instructional threads. The first is the building of a stable platform with the arms and shoulders at address, to remove unnecessary movement from the stroke. Horton Smith's box method fixes the arms at the sides and keeps the palms anchored opposite each other.[Fig. 6.5] This setup is similar to the one Marlene Hagge suggests in her tip, in which she extends her elbows slightly from her sides to create more of a pendulum action.[Fig. 6.6]

Another thread is the use of a single lever in the putting stroke.

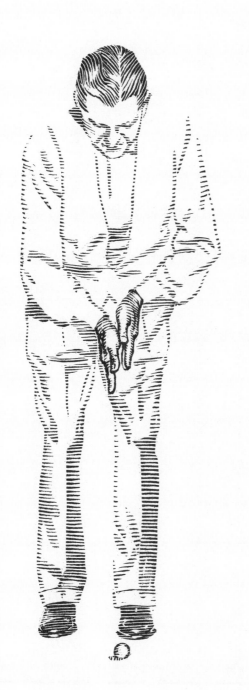

A. Ravielli

Three drawings—of Besselink from earlier, John Battini, and Dick Mayer—emphasize creating a solid base with the body and arms, using just the wrists to control the stroke. Battini emphasizes the need to grip the putter lightly, as if you were holding a bird in your hands,(Fig. 6.7) while Mayer's tip shows how the arms are anchored to the body on a 12-footer. The only real movement is the cocking and uncocking of the right wrist.(Fig. 6.8)

This "pop" putting method worked fairly well on the slow greens that were common on the PGA Tour in the 1950s, but has fallen out of style as putting surfaces have become faster. For example, the speed of the greens at the U.S. Open during the 1950s ran at approximately nine on the Stimpmeter—the same speed as the average public course today. PGA Tour courses now run 11 or 12, while greens at the U.S. Open or the Masters can get to 14.

It is no longer necessary to make aggressive contact to start the ball rolling on top of the longer grass. In addition, golf architecture has evolved; greens now have more undulations and steeper slopes. As a result, today's putting strokes place a premium on smoothness and distance control, because much less effort is required to make the ball travel the equivalent distance, and there is a real possibility of hitting putts too far and even off the greens.

Returning to Ravielli's era, the most elaborate of the putting drawings has the least to do with the stroke itself. Noble Chalfaunt's tip on green reading is fascinating for its use of three different full-body studies, in which Chalfaunt is using his putter as a gauge for the slope, marking his ball, and getting down close to the ground to see the putt's subtle break. The detail in the drawing is striking—from the spikes on the bottom of Chalfaunt's shoes to the folds on his pant leg.(Fig. 6.9)

6.6 Opposite: By extending her elbows, Marlene Hagge can make a unified, pendulum stroke.

A NEUTRAL PUTTING GRIP IS BEST I believe the best way to hold a putter is so it runs up the lifelines of your hands. That way, the shaft matches the plane of the forearms, and the putter works as an extension of the arms. This is different from a full-swing grip, in which the club sits across the palm, to allow the club to rotate around the body. I love this drawing, because there's nothing new being taught that's any better. –STAN UTLEY

6.7 No matter the type
of stroke, a light touch,
as if holding a bird in
your hands, is crucial for
creating touch around
the greens.

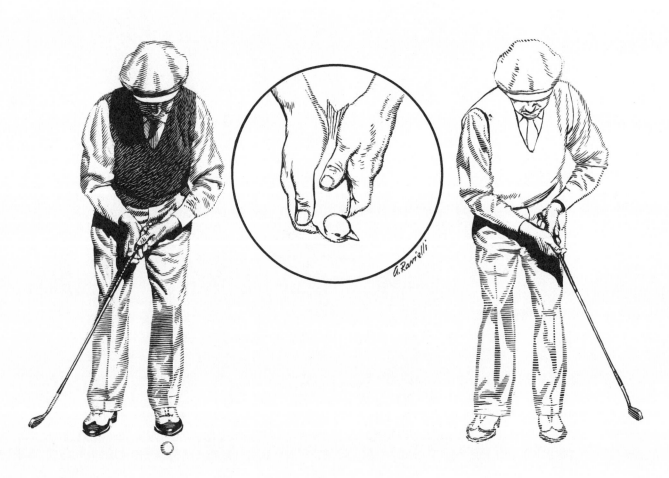

6.8 Dick Mayer has few
moving parts in his stroke.
The fewer moving parts
there are, the more consistent the stroke.

A. Ravielli

KEEP EYES OVER BALL TO SEE THE LINE Almost without exception, every great putter I've ever seen has set up with his or her eyes directly above the ball or slightly inside it, toward the feet. That's the best way to see the putt's line. –STAN UTLEY

A. Ravielli

The drawing of Chalfaunt's elaborate routine notwithstanding, simplicity is best in putting, then as now. Utley teaches neutral positions with the grip, posture, and stance, which don't influence the stroke one way or another. If the hands hang naturally and neutrally, they allow the putter to operate as an extension of the arms.

Utley wants to keep feel just as uncomplicated. Tossing a ball underhand to a target is an athletic move that doesn't require any thoughts about mechanics. Utley wants his students to putt that same way, relying on natural feel for tempo and distance, instead of thinking about manipulating the club.

Spend an afternoon trying some of these techniques and you'll quickly see how fickle the "art" of putting has been for players and teachers over the years. And even in an era when tour-caliber full swings look cloned, putting has retained a refreshing mix of styles and philosophies—which means if your method gets the ball in the hole, don't hesitate to keep using it.

6.9 Opposite: As Noble Chalfaunt shows, there are many ways to read the subtle breaks on a putting green.

A. Ravielli

CHIPPING |7| INSTRUCTION BY JIM McLEAN

CHIPPING | 7 |

INSTRUCTION
BY
JIM McLEAN

THE COMMON THEME throughout this series of chipping drawings is the importance of keeping the body stable. The chipping motion is controlled by the arms, and if other parts are moving, they disrupt the arms' ability to make consistent, crisp contact.

Simplicity is the goal: Essentially, the chipping strokes in these drawings are larger versions of a putting stroke, with a small pivot added. Amateurs complicate the motion and have problems because they try to manipulate the club, thinking they need to help the ball up in the air.

The drawing of Herman Herpel reinforces the idea that the chipping stroke should be as simple as possible, with the length of the backswing determining how far the ball will go. Herpel's hips pivot slightly toward the target during the swing, but otherwise the platform stays very stable. (Fig. 7.1)

A simple chipping motion has several virtues. It's easier to repeat, which translates into better distance control so chips end up closer to the hole. A simple motion is also easier to maintain in pressure situations. The face-on drawing of Marilyn Smith are striking (and not just because of her high heels!). There is no manipulation of the club by the hands, and the triangle created by the arms and shoulders stays intact

7.1 Opposite: The chipping stroke should be as simple as possible, with few moving parts. The length of the stroke determines how far the ball will travel.

KEEP BODY QUIET FOR CONSISTENCY The hands roll the club-face just slightly open in the backswing. Using mostly hands and wrists also elevates the clubhead quickly, setting up the proper downward strike. In addition, contact will be very precise because the body is so still and quiet.

Even with a super-short finish, the hips have rotated slightly toward the target. Notice the clubface is still held off—the toe of the clubhead has not turned over the heel. You can still see the left hand, while the head remains in the same position throughout the shot. –JIM McLEAN

A. Ravielli

TWO DIFFERENT RELEASES The smaller illustration shows a toe-up release, which produces a lower, running shot. The right hand has turned over the left hand and the first knuckle of the right index finger acts as a pointer. The right knee has kicked in slightly toward the target.

The main drawing shows the opposite release. I would call it a block release—the hands moving almost straight down the target line, with no wrist cock. Ravielli shows the ball in motion here—obviously, it flies high off the clubface. –JIM McLEAN

A. Ravielli

throughout, just as they do in a putting stroke. The ball just gets in the way as the club brushes the grass.(Fig. 7.2)

Besides changing the length of the backswing, another way to control distance is club selection. Tour players chip with anything from a sand wedge to a 7-iron, depending on how much carry and roll are required for the shot. The longer club will carry less and roll more; the wedges will do the opposite. At British Open courses, which have flat, firm turf, players sometimes hit 30-yard chips with mid-irons that roll most of the way to the hole, like a putt.

The most dramatic drawing in this chapter highlights Ravielli's skill. The Tom Watson montage shows the beginning of a full-swing backswing, along with the trajectory of a chip shot. Notice how Watson's clubface is still pointing up in his finish position, just like in the other drawings in this chapter. This shows that the hands have remained passive through impact, instead of flipping the club or turning it over. They're just holding on to the grip and transmitting power from the slight body turn and simple arm swing.(Fig. 7.3)

7.2 Opposite: Marilyn Smith makes a simple stroke and keeps her wrists firm through the stroke; there is no breakdown of the motion.

A. Ravielli

COCK RIGHT WRIST FOR CRISP CONTACT Here you see a very quiet body with the hands dominating the backswing—notice how much the right wrist is cocked. This allows the hands to remain over the ball while the clubhead travels much farther.

Impact is a classic "hit and hold" chip-shot release. The hands have stopped just after impact, and the clubhead has passed the grip. This would produce a low, running shot.

This is an example of a flip, or under, release. The head is down, and the body is dead still. The hands and wrists do almost all the work, which produces a high-trajectory shot with low spin. –JIM McLEAN

A. Ravielli

[CHIPPING]

189

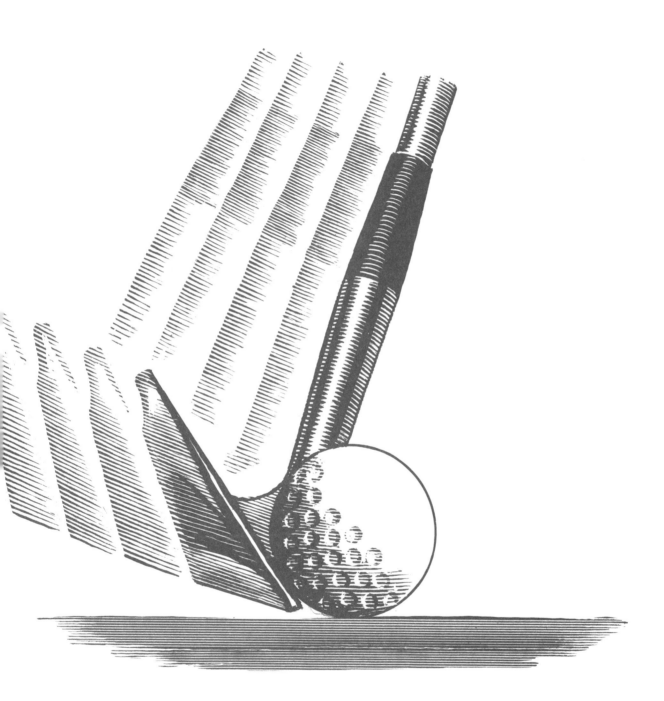

PITCHING | **8** | INSTRUCTION BY RAY FLOYD

PITCHING |8| INSTRUCTION BY RAY FLOYD

THE SINGLE BIGGEST DIFFERENCE between how a tour player and a 20-handicapper hit pitch shots can be neatly summarized by the close-up drawing of a wedge at impact.[(Fig. 8.6)] The club is approaching the ball on a descending path, which is what good players do on every shot except with the driver. Poor players think they need to help the ball into the air, flipping or scooping the clubhead so it is traveling up at impact. That's a fatal move that produces stubs, chili-dips, weak bleeders to the right, and bladed shots.

Once a player masters the descending path, the next challenge is distance control—figuring out which combination of club selection and swing length produces, say, a 50-yard shot instead of a 40-yard one.

Good distance control is largely a function of feel, and many of the drawings in this chapter attempt to give golfers a feel-based key. Al Mengert's tip is a perfect example. Ravielli's drawing connects the image of an underhand toss—a familiar movement to most—to the length of a swing for a pitch shot. A longer toss would require a longer follow-through; the same is true for a pitch shot.[(Fig. 8.1)]

Pat Devany uses her watch face to demonstrate the proper pitch technique. If the face points to the sky, the swing is too flat, causing a downswing path that is shallow, not descending. If the face looks down,

8.1 Opposite: To keep things simple, think of the length of the pitching motion as an underhand toss, an act that nearly everybody can relate to.

it means the clubface is closed, which will result in low, unpredictable shots. In a good, compact pitching backswing, the club goes back in an upright position, so the shaft is nearly vertical from a down-the-line view. As Devany demonstrates, this position causes her watch dial to face at about 45 degrees. This kind of visual cue is a common teaching technique that works well with some kinds of learners.[Fig. 8.2]

The remaining three drawings in this chapter illustrate more advanced, specialty pitches. Nowadays, the 60-degree wedge makes it easy to hit a high, soft shot. But in Marlene Hagge's era, players either had to open the face of the pitching wedge or hit the shot like Hagge demonstrates here—with the ball well forward in the stance so it is off the left instep, and with plenty of wrist action in both the backswing and follow-through. Unfortunately, it's a dangerous shot to teach beginners because of their tendency to scoop with the right wrist instead of rotating it through, as Hagge does.[Fig. 8.3]

Al Esposito demonstrates two different kinds of recovery pitches in the remaining drawings. In the first, he shows how widening the stance and turning the left foot out on an uphill pitch promotes a bigger swing and a fuller finish—critical for shots that have enough energy to make it over the slope and reach the hole.[Fig. 8.4] In the other, Esposito shows how a pitch from a sandy lie in the rough is more like a bunker shot than a standard pitch. He uses an open stance and hits an inch behind the ball, as he would on a long explosion shot.[Fig. 8.5]

8.3 Before lob wedges became widespread, players like Marlene Hagge used plenty of wrist action to add loft to the wedge, a technique that has fallen out of use.

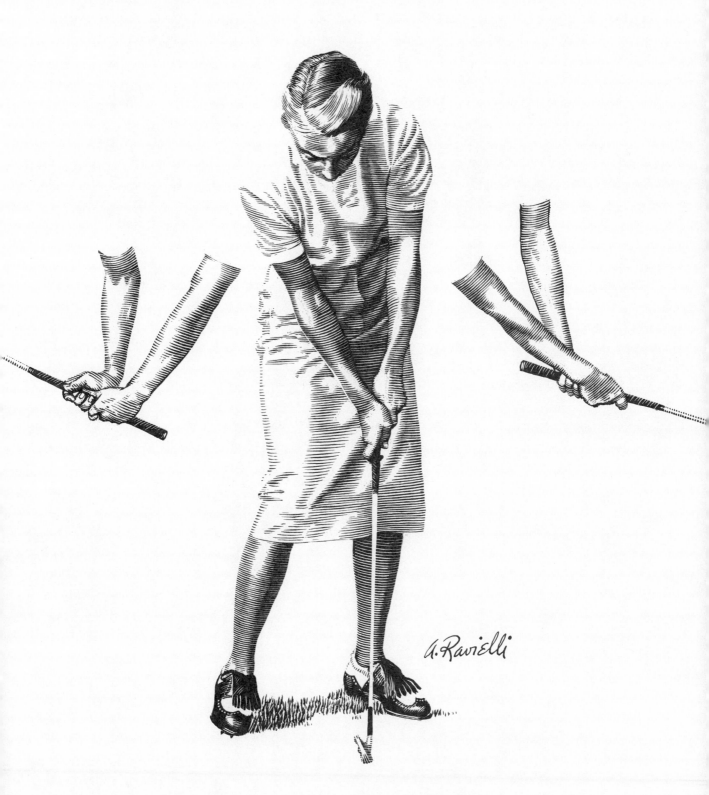

[PITCHING]

197

8.4 An uphill pitch
requires a couple of adjustments: a wider stance and
a bigger swing.

8.5 A pitch from a
sandy lie is similar to an
explosion shot from a
bunker, in which the club
hits the ground behind
the ball.

CONTROL DISTANCE WITH SWING'S LENGTH Art Wall is demonstrating the classic pitch-and-run technique here—no wrist break through impact. Because this swing doesn't have a lot of moving parts, it is very consistent, and you can dial in distance with the length of the motion, as you would with the putter. –RAY FLOYD

8.6 HIT DOWN ON THE BALL TO CREATE BACKSPIN I conduct 15 short-game clinics a year, and the first question I always get is about creating backspin. One way to think of it is to compare it to hitting a drop shot in tennis. You put backspin on that shot by cutting down on the ball as hard as you can. In golf, you impart backspin by keeping the ball on the grooves for as long as possible. Doing that requires a crisp, downward strike with a wristy stroke—hitting the ball first, not the grass. –RAY FLOYD

SAND SHOTS | 9 | INSTRUCTION BY RAY FLOYD AND BOB TOSKI

SAND SHOTS |9|

INSTRUCTION
BY RAY FLOYD
AND BOB TOSKI

ANTHONY RAVIELLI was best able to use imagery when illustrating greenside bunker shots. Because the technique required to hit an explosion shot is different from any other, it's difficult to describe with words alone. But Ravielli perfectly captured the idea of hitting the sand first and sending the ball out on a cushion of sand in his drawing of Johnny Revolta. By illustrating the divot of sand needed to hit the shot correctly, Ravielli immediately gave the reader a sense of how long the motion should be. Since the two most common mistakes from the bunker are hitting the ball first and digging the leading edge of the clubhead into the sand too far behind the ball, the simplicity of this image is priceless.[(Fig. 9.1)]

The drawing of Phil Taylor takes the imagery to the next level. The inset drawings show the impact point in the sand, as well as the amount of sand displaced. The top inset represents a standard explosion shot, which flies shorter and has less spin. The second inset is for a longer shot that has more height and spin, which requires the club to hit closer to the ball and take less sand.[(Fig. 9.2)]

Two other drawings in this chapter can offer immediate assistance to the average player. In one, Fred Novak shows how most average players set up for an explosion shot: feet square to the target line and the club-

9.1 Opposite: Ravielli was able to capture the idea of sending the ball out of a bunker on a cushion of sand.

9.2 The length of the shot depends on how much sand the golfer displaces. The longer the shot, the less sand he takes.

a. Ravielli

9.3 The standard explosion shot requires adjustments like an open clubface and an open stance, as Fred Novak shows on the right. On the left, Novak shows how most amateurs perform the shot incorrectly, with a square face and stance.

A. Ravielli

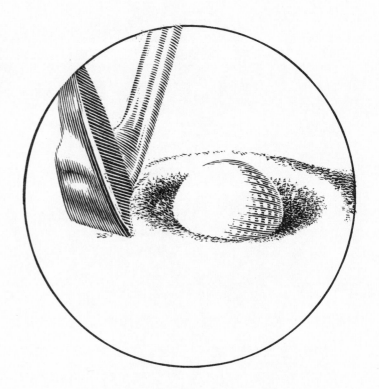

9.4 HANDLING A BURIED LIE I don't think any current player would hit a shot from a fried egg lie this way—it looks like he has a pitching wedge or even a 9-iron. I'd use a sand wedge, open the clubface, and try to hit more behind the ball and get under it. That way, the ball comes out higher and lands softer.

The technique shown here tends to make the ball knuckle and roll a lot more. Why would players from this era have hit the shot this way? Well, it's certainly not because they didn't have the right equipment. Recently, I saw a classic Gene Sarazen sand wedge from the '30s, and it's basically the same club we have now.
–RAY FLOYD

[SAND SHOTS]

G. Ravielli

9.5 SET UP BEHIND THE BALL In the larger drawing, Fred Hawkins is looking about two or three inches behind the ball, which is the standard way to hit a bunker shot. His left arm is straight, but his left wrist is slightly cupped. His right arm is bent and almost resting against his hip. Together, the arms really give the feel that he's going to hit under the ball and get it up in the air. Hawkins's clubface is aligned slightly right, open to the line of play, and his weight is well on his right side—a preprogrammed setup to undercut the ball and throw the ball up in the air, along with a long, shallow divot of sand. One thing we can't overlook is that he has to keep the left arm moving through impact—not stop it. Otherwise, he'll pull it or chunk it.

In the smaller picture, his head is more centered over the ball. He's trying to pinch the ball out of a bad lie in the sand. The ball position, weight distribution, and the position of his arms and legs have changed. He's trying to hit much closer to the ball on this shot, to dig it out of this fried egg lie. –BOB TOSKI

9.6 Opposite: In the smaller image, Helen Dettweiler illustrates a common fault: overswinging. As she shows in the main image, a shorter backswing and an accelerating downswing are enough to displace the sand and send the ball softly onto the green.

face square. The shot is easier to hit with both an open stance and club-face. These adjustments allow the clubhead to slide under the ball, producing a high shot with slight left-to-right spin.[Fig. 9.3]

In the other drawing, Walter Burkemo demonstrates one way to blast a half-buried ball out of a bunker. Normally, you'd want to use the bounce on the bottom of the sand wedge to slide the clubhead through the sand. In this case, Burkemo intentionally digs the leading edge of the club (most likely a pitching wedge, which has very little bounce and a sharp leading edge) into the sand just behind the crater created by the ball. The goal is to make a hard swing and really propel the ball out of its crater, even if the ball runs too far on the green.[Fig. 9.4]

Fred Hawkins's tip is more subtle, but also very helpful for the average player. Head position at address goes a long way toward determining the bottom of the swing. By moving his head slightly away from the target so it is over his right instep, Hawkins makes it easier for the club to enter the sand behind the ball. If his head were more toward the target, he would shift the bottom of the swing forward, increasing the likelihood of striking the ball directly with the club and sending the shot screaming over the green.[Fig. 9.5]

Helen Dettweiler makes an often overlooked point in her tip. Many players make a big backswing on a medium-length bunker shot and lose feel for the clubhead. Or worse, they decelerate in the downswing, which prevents the clubhead from having enough force to cut through the sand. For most explosion shots, a shoulder-height backswing is big enough, as long as it leads to an assertive, accelerating downswing.[Fig. 9.6]

LEGENDS | **10** | LESSONS FROM GOLF'S ALL-TIME GREATS

Three of golf's legends, as
immortalized by Ravielli:
Ben Hogan, Jack Nicklaus,
Tom Watson.

LEGENDS |10| LESSONS FROM GOLF'S ALL-TIME GREATS

ALTHOUGH HE WOULD NEVER ADMIT or even think it, Anthony Ravielli himself has become a legend through his work with other legends of the game. And the book that established Ravielli's stature was Ben Hogan's *Five Lessons*.

As Curt Sampson writes in *Hogan*, "With its specificity and detail, and with Ravielli's medical-illustration drawings, *Five Lessons* became the *Gray's Anatomy* of golf. At last the sports instructors had a manual, and teach-yourselfers had a roadmap."

Although Ravielli always will be remembered for *Five Lessons*, he considered his collaborations with two other legends, Bobby Jones and Tom Watson, to be just as significant and considered every moment working with them to be pleasure-filled enlightening experiences.

Although quite different in their approaches to instruction and in their personalities, each influenced golfers for generations, helped by Ravielli's visual interpretations of their words. But in the end, Ravielli was more than an illustrator of these legends' books. He became their friend and partner in the dissemination of their thoughts about the game.

There are many different ways a golfer can become a legend. In the case of Bobby Jones, a man who retired from the game in 1930 at age 28 after being the only man to ever win the Grand Slam (U.S. Open, British Open, British Amateur, and U.S. Amateur), legend hardly describes Jones's impact on golf.

The embodiment of grace, Jones represents all that's exceptional in a person and is the personification of the intrinsic values of golf. Bobby Jones essentially defined what it means to be a gentleman, possess decorum, have consideration for your fellow opponent and players, and to be honest and have a sense of fair play.

Jones's character, even later in life, was such that Ravielli reveled in working with him. "I treasure my time with Jones and my correspondence with him, which I saved," Ravielli told *The Met Golfer* in 1990. Of course, Ravielli was hardly the only figure to be moved by Jones's game and grace. Jack Nicklaus was aware of Jones's legacy almost from the first time he picked up a golf club.

"I never got to see Bob Jones play a golf shot, but I played a lot of 'golf' with him," says Nicklaus, who broke Jones's record of 13 majors. "Jones won the 1926 U.S. Open at Scioto Country Club, the club I grew up on, and all I ever heard was what Jones did on this hole, or where he hit his drive on that hole. He was a hero at my house.

"So it was a thrill to meet Mr. Jones for the first time, when I was 15 and playing in my first U.S. Amateur. Before the tournament he said he was going to follow me for a few holes. When he showed up on the 11th hole, I got so nervous that I went bogey-bogey-double bogey to go from 1 up to 2 down. It's one of my favorite memories in golf."

Jones's swing was as graceful as he was off the course, and Ravielli was able to capture not only Jones's technical brilliance but also his fluidity and rhythm. These sketches show the sense of effortless tempo that many find hypnotic, even today.

"Jones's swing was long and rhythmic—a very pretty golf swing," Nicklaus says. "When he played, golf wasn't a power game. Jones's swing was a timing swing, designed to create

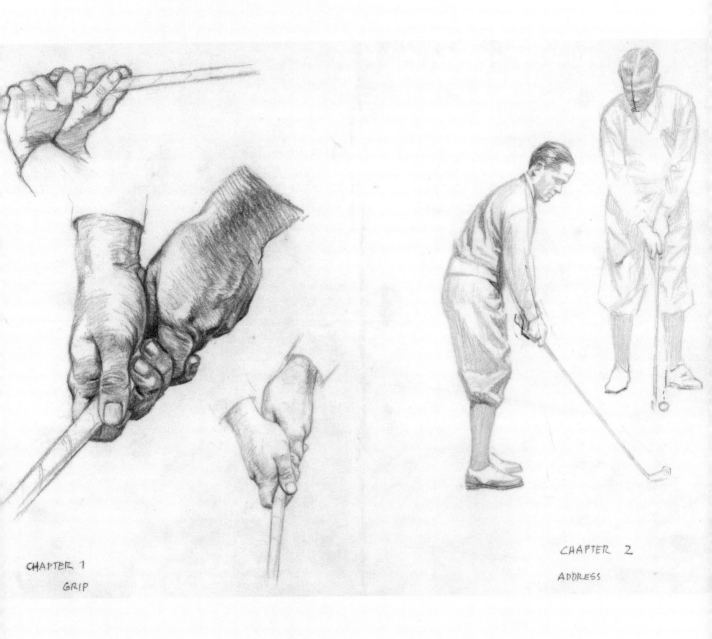

CHAPTER 1
GRIP

CHAPTER 2
ADDRESS

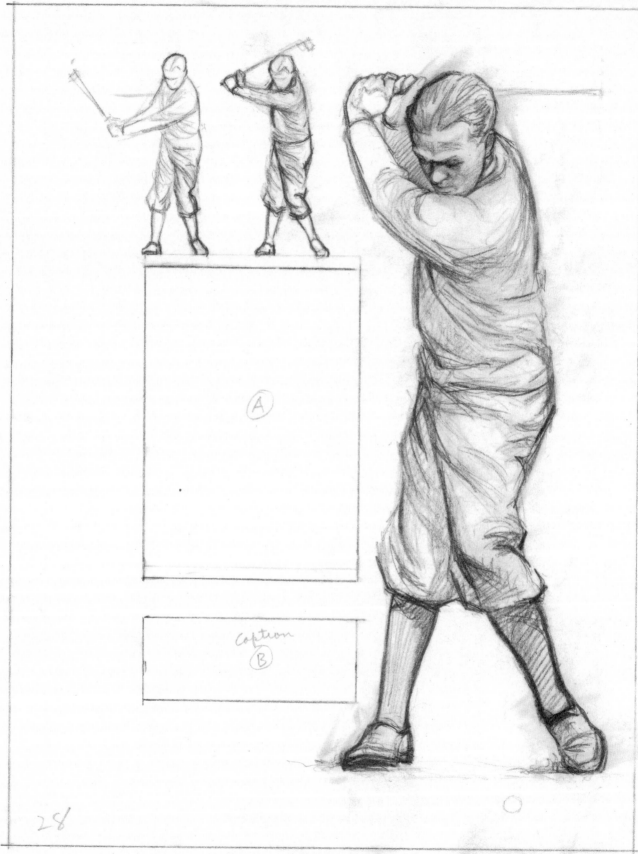

A

Caption
B

28

49

CHAPTER 4

CHAPTER 7

CHAPTER 8

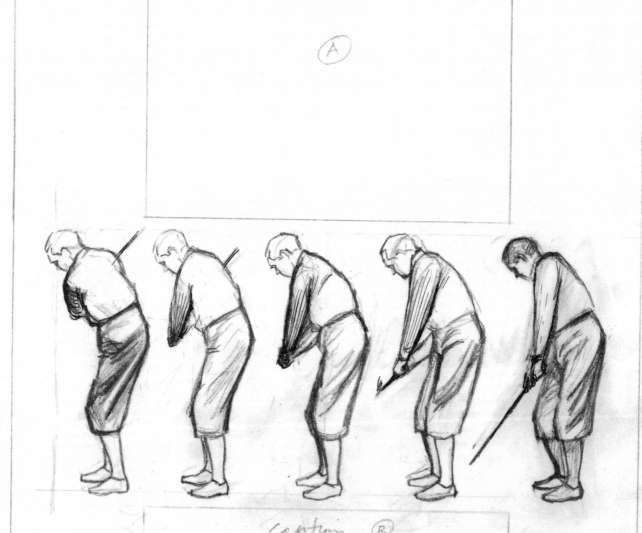

(A)

Caption (B)

40

consistent, solid contact. It had to be that way, because of the equipment he was using—flexible hickory shafts and small, unforgiving clubheads.

"My swing was shaped by the equipment I played as well. Players of today have swings designed to create power. They're trying to make a wider arc and get more leverage to hit the ball as far as they can, and the equipment helps them do that. Ernie Els is the one modern player who has that same flowing, effortless look—but he's definitely creating a lot of power."

Spanning the generations, another legend with whom Ravielli formed a close bond and affection was Tom Watson. Whenever his name is mentioned in the Ravielli household, a common element arises among Georgia and her children: a smile.

Watson and Ravielli, along with Nick Seitz, were longtime collaborators. It was a harmonious relationship based on each person's contribution to the project, along with the respect each held for the other's talents. According to Georgia, Watson was Ravielli's favorite golfer to work with. There was an underlying understanding that made them a true team, each a master in his respective craft while truly appreciating the other's talent.

When asked to describe why he selected Ravielli to work with on *Strategic Golf* and *Getting Up and Down*, Watson said, "There was no other choice if you wanted the best. His skills were perfection and accuracy his hallmark."

"Tony would always say, 'What a gentlemen Tom was,'" Georgia says. Fittingly, those are the same words Watson uses to describe Ravielli.

CHAPTER ~~14~~ 14

CHAPTER ~~13~~
13

CHAPTER 12

Tom Watson and Anthony
Ravielli held a mutual
respect and admiration for
each other, and Ravielli's
illustration of Watson's
swing arc shows the power
and grace of the five-time
British Open champion.

Above: Ravielli brought home Watson's 1983 British Open trophy, and he was stopped at customs by a disbelieving official.

When I asked Watson to describe Ravielli, I could hear an underlying tone of respect in his response. How often does one of the greatest golfers of the century choose the word love—"We all loved Tony"—to describe an illustrator? As well as phrases like "kind, true gentlemen; a man of manners," which are so rare. Again, these are the same words Georgia used to describe Ravielli's feelings and thoughts for Watson.

Of course, there were the times Ravielli had difficulty illustrating Watson's hair on the scratchboard. But as a master of his craft, Ravielli wouldn't let go until he captured the exact representation of the moment and man.

As seen in the photograph of Watson and Ravielli exchanging the 1983 British Open trophy from Royal Birkdale in Ravielli's backyard, smiles abounded throughout their relationship. Georgia recounted the famous trip in which Watson asked Ravielli to take the claret jug home right after his fifth British Open victory. "You could only imagine how nervous Tony was," she says. "When he came through customs, he was stopped with the gigantic trophy in his possession. Customs found it hard to believe anyone would part with such a triumph." But Watson had entrusted Ravielli with the safekeeping of his treasure, a testimony to their relationship, as deeply rooted as the century-old trophy.

AFTERWORD

IT IS NO ACCIDENT that the most important photograph and illustration in golf history depict the same man. Hy Peskin's shot of Ben Hogan's 1-iron into the last green at Merion in the 1950 U.S. Open is a study in athletic poetry, revered for its distillation of golf's greatest ball-striker. The artwork, of course, that stands above every other drawing or painting is Tony Ravielli's depiction of a pane of glass that extends magically from Hogan's neck and shoulders to the ball at address in the most important golf instruction book ever published, Hogan's *Five Lessons*.

Forgive me for this digression: Recently I was in the home of a leading teacher discussing the swing change that Tiger Woods was immersed in. The subject of swing plane is at the core of Tiger's reconstruction. His previous coach, Butch Harmon, learned at the feet of his father, Claude, who was a Hogan contemporary and friend. His current coach, Hank Haney, is a student of Hogan's theories, but broke with him over swing plane and the Ravielli depiction. As the discussion turned heated, I realized we were debating a half-century-old piece of art. In the room was not only the ghost of Hogan, but here, too, resurrected was that old, flannel-shirted, pipe-puffing, half-blind artist himself.

Knowing how Tony worked, I always suspected he was more than a little responsible for the pane-of-glass imagery. I can picture him standing quietly in the background while Hogan explained swing plane to the book's coauthor, Herbert Warren Wind, who no doubt was taking meticulous notes on his yellow legal pads. When Hogan would grip a club to demonstrate, I imagine Tony unobtrusively holding up his movie camera and filming the motion. (Years later, Tony came to a *Golf Digest* editorial meeting and showed us these silent films while the audience sat

GOLF DIGEST

$1.50
March 1982
One million
circulation,
largest of
any golfing
publication

HOGAN
vs
NICKLAUS
vs
WATSON

Learn from our
total analysis
of their games

Plus a pullout
comparison
of the 3 great
modern swings

A. Ravielli

enraptured as if the Rosetta stone itself had been placed on the conference table.) Because I'd seen it happen so many times with other instruction articles authored by Byron Nelson, Tom Watson, and countless others, I believe it is more than likely that the concept of swing plane as "a pane of glass" originated not with Hogan or Wind but with Ravielli. It is precisely the kind of riveting essence that the artist spent a lifetime communicating dramatically, memorably, without words.

Why is the pane of glass so significant? It embodies the science of Hogan's mystical approach to the swing. Ravielli expanded our vocabulary with his drawings of pronation and supination, but it was his capture of Hogan's swing plane that remains the enduring image of golf instruction.

I guess you could argue that Ravielli's other scratchboard illustration of Hogan's swing face-on at impact, which has served in various forms over five decades as the symbol of the Ben Hogan Company, was reproduced more often. Hogan owned the copyright of the book and all its editorial contents. I once asked Tony if he'd ever been paid for its commercial use as a corporate logo, thinking in modern terms that a hard-nosed IMG agent would have made him millions. That Ravielli hadn't been paid a cent is not so telling of his gentle soul as that it never even occurred to him to wonder.

Jerry Tarde
Chairman and Editor-in-Chief, *Golf Digest*
March 2005

ACKNOWLEDGEMENTS AND CONTRIBUTORS

ACKNOWLEDGEMENTS

So many people have given their time, talent, and energy to bring *Classic Golf Instruction* to fruition. I would like to thank Georgia Ravielli for sharing her intimate thoughts and her life with Tony. Her warmth, generosity of spirit, and reflections brought to life the magnificent works of Anthony Ravielli for generations to come. In addition, I would like thank Ellen, Jane, and Tony, Jr. for sharing their childhood memories of their father.

Family and friends always play an amazing role. Sandra McConnell's loving support and constant presence in my daily life made each moment more enjoyable. My mother and father, Robin and Robin, provided me with the solid foundation to realize my dreams, and also never left my side among my many journeys. Their love, guidance, and friendship couldn't be greater than mine is for them. I would also like to thank Dr. Laura Singer, whose vast knowledge of the inner self opened doors never before seen.

This book would not be possible without my grandfather, Dr. Robin C. Obetz, who was not only my childhood best friend, but my mentor and fellow lover of the game of golf. Had it not been for his constant search for the perfect swing and his comprehensive golf-book collection, I would never have seen *Five Lessons* and known what I was staring at 30 years later.

I would also like to offer a special thanks Jim Halperin and Alex during the acquisition phase. You were true gentlemen and men of great integrity.

A BIG thanks goes to the incredible support and wealth of history provided by *Golf Digest*'s Jerry Tarde, Bob Carney, and Nick Seitz. Their combined efforts surpass generosity. It has been extraordinary to listen to their insights into the game, along with their unique experiences with Tony and his art.

Matthew Rudy, a *Golf Digest* editor and instructional writer for *Classic Golf Instruction*, deserves tremendous credit for his ability to work with the incredible group of teaching and tour professionals who consulted to the book. You were a pleasure to work with, and full of amazing analysis of each drawing.

Many, many thanks go out to the teaching and tour pros who were kind enough to lend their wisdom to the Ravielli drawings. I would like to offer my sincere thanks to Jack Nicklaus for his lifelong devotion to the purity of the game and for sharing his thoughts about a purist the game's art. You and Tony shared the same love and respect for golf. May the legacy of Anthony Ravielli and each pro's comments about the illustrations survive for all golfers to enjoy, learn, and try for themselves.

To the entire Rizzoli team: Ellen Nidy, Anet Sirna-Bruder, editor Hunki Yun, and designer John Klotnia. Many thanks for your creativity and daily efforts to ensure each detail came through. Most importantly, thanks to publisher Charles Miers, who instantly recognized Ravielli's art as a significant contribution to the landscape of golf and provided a forum for allowing the world to see the scartchboards in their true glory. Charles, your vision and commitment to *Classic Golf Instruction* were a true gift for both the art world and for all golfers searching to find their own brand of swing.

Christopher R. Obetz

CONTRIBUTORS

CHUCK COOK: The 1996 PGA of America Teacher of the Year, Cook has taught U.S. Open winners Corey Pavin, Tom Kite, and the late Payne Stewart. Cook, who is based at the Barton Creek Resort in Austin, Tex., is a *Golf Digest* Teaching Professional.

JIM FLICK: The 1998 PGA of America Teacher of the Year, Flick has taught hundreds of tour pros, most notably Jack Nicklaus. Based at Desert Mountain in Scottsdale, Ariz., Flick is a *Golf Digest* Teaching Professional.

RAY FLOYD: Floyd won 22 PGA Tour events, including four major championships: the 1969 and 1982 PGA Championships, the 1976 Masters, and the 1986 U.S. Open. He is one of just two players to win on the PGA Tour and the Champions Tour in the same year.

HANK HANEY: Currently Tiger Woods's instructor, Haney also has taught Mark O'Meara and Hank Kuehne and is the 1993 PGA of America Teacher of the Year. Haney, who owns several facilities in Texas, is a *Golf Digest* Teaching Professional.

BUTCH HARMON: The son of 1948 Masters champion Claude Harmon, Harmon has taught Greg Norman, Tiger Woods, and Adam Scott. He owns the Butch Harmon School of Golf outside Las Vegas. Harmon is a *Golf Digest* Teaching Professional.

DAVID LEADBETTER: Based at the David Leadbetter Golf Academy in Orlando, Fla., Leadbetter has worked with some of the best players in the world, including Ernie Els, Nick Faldo, Nick Price, Lee Westwood, and Se Ri Pak. Leadbetter, a *Golf Digest* Teaching Professional, is the author of *The Fundamentals of Hogan*.

MIKE McGETRICK: The owner of the Mike McGetrick Golf Academy in Denver, McGetrick has taught many top LPGA Tour players, including Hall of Famers Juli Inkster and Beth Daniel. The 1999 PGA of America Teacher of the Year, McGetrick is a *Golf Digest* Teaching Professional.

JIM McLEAN: Based at the Jim McLean Golf Academy at the Doral Resort and Spa in Miami, McLean is the 1994 PGA of America Teacher of the Year. A *Golf Digest* Teaching Professional, McLean has taught PGA Tour players Brad Faxon and Len Mattiace, as well as LPGA Tour pro Cristie Kerr.

TOM NESS: Ness teaches at the Chateau Elan Winery and Resort in Braselton, Ga. Ness, a *Golf Digest* Teaching Professional, coached actor Jim Caviezel for his role as Bobby Jones in *Bobby Jones: Strokes of Genius*.

GREG NORMAN: The winner of more than 80 tournaments world-wide, including the 1986 and 1993 British Opens, Norman was the No. 1 player in the world for 331 weeks in the '80s and '90s, a record recently broken by Tiger Woods.

RANDY SMITH: The head professional at Royal Oaks Golf Club in Dallas, Smith has been named both the PGA of America Teacher of the Year and Professional of the Year. Smith, a *Golf Digest* Teaching Professional, has taught PGA Tour players Justin Leonard and Harrison Frazar.

RICK SMITH: The owner of the Treetops Resort in Gaylord, Mich., Smith has taught numerous PGA Tour players, including Phil Mickelson, Lee Janzen, and Rocco Mediate. In addition to his work as an instructor, Smith is also a successful golf course designer.

BILL STINES: Stines is the head professional at Scioto Country Club in Columbus, Ohio, which is the course Jack Nicklaus grew up playing.

DR. JIM SUTTIE: The 2000 PGA of America Teacher of the Year, Dr. Suttie has worked with dozens of tour players, including Fred Funk, Loren Roberts, and Steve Flesch. Suttie, who has a doctorate in bio-mechanics from Middle Tennessee State, operates the Dr. Jim Suttie Golf Academy at The Club at TwinEagles in Naples, Fla.

BOB TOSKI: One of the top players of his day, Toski led the PGA Tour money list in 1954. But he retired early to spend more time with his family and became an instructor, teaching pros like Tom Kite and Judy Rankin. Toski also was a cofounder of the *Golf Digest* Schools.

STAN UTLEY: A former tour player, Utley specializes in short-game instruction and teaches many tour players, including Jay Haas, Craig Stadler, and Peter Jacobsen. Utley holds the PGA Tour record for fewest putts for nine holes, with six.

MATTHEW RUDY is a senior writer at *Golf Digest*, where he has collaborated on magazine pieces with Ernie Els, Phil Mickelson, Johnny Miller, Hank Haney, Butch Harmon, and David Leadbetter, among others. A former golf reporter at *Sports Illustrated*, he is also the author of *Golf Digest Perfect Your Swing*, *Breaking 90 with Johnny Miller*, and *Complete Idiot's Guide to Golf*, with Michelle McGann.

CHAPTER 4